Sussex Top ~~~~

The picturesque north-east end of Chichester Harbour from Dell Quay.

David Bathurst

Photographs by David Bathurst

S.B. Publications

To Ellen

By the same author:

The Selsey Tram
Six of the Best!
The Jennings Companion
Around Chichester In Old Photographs
Financial Penalties - Enforcement in Magistrates' Courts
Here's A Pretty Mess!
Magisterial Lore
The Beaten Track
Poetic Justice
Walking the Coastline of Sussex
Best Sussex Walks
Let's Take It From The Top
Walking the Disused Railways of Sussex

Contributions to:
Introduction to *While I Remember* - autobiography of Anthony Buckeridge
The Encyclopaedia of Boys' School Stories

First published in 2005 by S.B. Publications
19 Grove Road, Seaford, East Sussex BN25 1TP

ISBN 1-85770-309-X

Typeset by EH Graphics, East Sussex (01273) 515527
Printed by Ethos Productions Ltd.

CONTENTS

ABOUT THE AUTHOR

David Bathurst was born in Guildford in 1959 and has enjoyed writing and walking all his adult life. He has written fourteen books, four of which have been about Sussex, most recently *Walking The Disused Railways Of Sussex* which was published by SB Publications in 2004. David also enjoys performing, and in 2004 achieved the unusual feat of reciting all the Gilbert and Sullivan operas from memory. He works as a senior legal advisor to magistrates sitting at Chichester and Worthing and lives just a few miles outside Chichester with his wife Susan and daughter Jennifer.

The lovely chapel of St. Wilfrid close to the shores of Pagham Harbour and immortalised by Rudyard Kipling.

INTRODUCTION

One of the most popular reference books of recent years has been *The Top Ten Of Everything,* listing the top ten of a huge number of categories, ranging from religious belief and natural wonders to films and TV programmes. This book aims to provide a similar collection of lists of Top Tens, but all specifically related to Sussex or, more precisely, the counties of East and West Sussex and the city of Brighton and Hove.

Obviously the categories appropriate to a book of lists of Top Tens for Sussex must be dictated by the character, the architecture, the geography and the people of that county. Happily, Sussex offers so many interesting and contrasting landscapes, buildings, experiences, pastimes and amenities that there is no shortage of categories and there are, in most cases, far more than ten nominees for each category. The book provides 30 categories in all, offering hopefully something for everybody. Holidaymakers and day trippers can plan their itineraries around the selections of historic towns and villages, houses, castles, museums and gardens. Parents wanting to entertain their children for the day need look no further than the Family Days Out category. Walkers and nature-lovers will be guided by the Top Ten rivers, named footpaths, viewpoints, coastal wonders and places to watch birds. It is, however, more than just a guide book for visitors. Categories devoted to ghosts, disasters, weather extremes and eyesores shed light on the less appealing aspects of the history and character of Sussex, and eccentric aspects of the county are not overlooked either, with lists of bizarre place names and landmarks. The whole book is a mine of information and interest not just for those requiring practical guidance on planning a day out or holiday in Sussex, but for those wanting to know more about the very best – and in some cases the very worst – that the county can offer. It is at once a handy reference book and a browser's paradise.

Choice of Top Ten For Each Category

Although in making my selection I have been guided very much by established reference works, any choice must, of course, be subjective. Each category has required me to apply different "yardsticks;" in the case of golf courses, pubs and restaurants, for example, I have looked for their inclusion in at least two of the established guides to the best of them; for churches, I have looked to Simon Jenkins' monumental *England's Thousand Best Churches* and his star ratings in that work; for windmills I have relied on the judgment of Nikolaus Pevsner coupled with Brunnarius' unparalleled guide to the windmills of Sussex. Top tens of some categories have almost defined themselves: although one might expect Sussex to be richly blessed with castles, the ten chosen are the only ten castles of significance in Sussex of which any trace remains. Being a keen walker and tearoom buff, I consider my own judgment of such categories as Top Ten Tearooms and Named Footpaths to have been sufficient! All other things being equal, I have tried to achieve an even split between East and West Sussex but I have NOT consciously sought to include five from East and five from West Sussex in each category. Some categories seem to have produced far more entries from one than from the other. For instance, West Sussex seems to have the lion's share of the top ten pubs. I promise that my own place of residence, in West Sussex, has had no bearing on this!! Inevitably there is some overlap between categories; rather like the BAFTA awards where the same film or TV star may go up to the podium two or three times in one night, some locations in this book crop up more than once in different categories, and I have not omitted an entry from a given category simply because that place has featured elsewhere. Beachy Head, for instance, excels as a viewpoint, a place to watch birds and a coastal wonder, and I think it is right to include it in all three of those categories. By the same token, some locations may be get an entry of their own under one category but are merely mentioned "in passing" in another because of the nature of the category in question: an example is Lewes Castle which is a Top Ten Castle in its own right but must logically also be mentioned when considering the various aspects of Lewes as a Top Ten Historic Town.

However and wherever my choices are categorised, I must obviously accept that some readers will vehemently disagree with some of them. "Why on earth did that brilliant pub we ate in yesterday not get in?"..... "We ate at one of the supposed Top Ten restaurants and the food and service were awful...." And so on. All that said, half the fun of a book of this kind is to provoke friendly debate as to which are the best pubs, restaurants, gardens etc in Sussex, and if you wish to share your ideas with me, through my publishers, I should love to hear them. I must also accept the danger that a particularly good establishment will change hands or go out of business; a guide book of this nature can never be absolutely up-to-date although all the information was, to the best of my knowledge, accurate as at July 2005. Through my publishers, I would like to be made aware of errors so that things can be put right for any reprint.

How To Use The Book

As I have stated, the book can be enjoyed as much by the armchair traveller as by those using it as a practical guide. There is no magic to the sequence in which the categories are set out; I have deliberately aimed to make it a book to dip into, rather than to be read from cover to cover. The one-to-ten list under each category is usually in alphabetical order of location. The subject of the entry is in bold and this is followed by the location and, where applicable, a contact number. Full postal addresses, postcodes and opening times are generally not included in the interests of space, on the basis that using the contact number will facilitate the provision of the further details required. I have endeavoured to provide contact numbers for all entries which I feel require them. The descriptions attaching to each entry are necessarily brief and do not pretend to do full justice to the locations or things being described, but again I am limited by space. There are 3 stars against one entry in each category, signifying that that is in my view the most outstanding of the ten entries – again based on the opinion of others and my own personal experiences.

My Thanks

I would like to extend my thanks to all the library and tourist information staff whom I have approached for information and leaflets to help me compile this book; to Lindsay at SB Publications for her support, advice and encouragement; and to my wife Susan and my daughter Jennifer, who accompanied me on many of my fact-finding missions with little or no protest!!

David Bathurst
Woodgate
2005

Naughty but nice: delicious Sussex cream teas await at Robsons in Lewes.

TOP TEN TEA PLACES IN SUSSEX

The Singing Kettle, 6 *Waterloo Square, Alfriston, East Sussex, tel 01323 870723*

This pretty tea room stands at one end of the town's attractive market square, and there is a choice between sitting in the quaint cottagey interior with its white-plastered walls and redbrick fireplace, looking out at the activity on the square, or going into the garden at the back. A good range of teas includes Assam, Earl Grey, Chai, Darjeeling and Peppermint; savoury fare includes cheese, garlic and herb paté with warm toasted pitta bread, home-made salmon fishcakes with parsley sauce, bacon buck rarebit with organic bread, large cheese scone served with mature cheddar and apple and date chutney, and spinach, parsley and cheese rice bake with mixed salad; while for the sweet-toothed there is warm treacle and coconut tart with cream, gooseberry crumble and custard, a range of cream teas and, for those colder winter days, hot buttered crumpets.

The Singing Kettle in the lovely village of Alfriston is a traditional tea room serving delicious hot and cold food.

Belinda's, *13 Tarrant Street, Arundel, West Sussex, tel 01903 882977*
The atmosphere and décor of this tearoom, housed in a 16th century building, is quintessentially English with its roaring fire, rustic wooden furnishings, low beams, brasses and lovely blue and white crockery. Even the biggest appetites will be satisfied by such specials as steamed homemade steak and kidney pudding, sandwiches stuffed with ham, beef or lamb, roast of the day, savoury omelettes and traditional puddings such as jam or syrup sponge. Lighter meals include the Savoury Tea, consisting of two cheese scones served with cream cheese and celery, while the less diet-conscious may tuck into one of Belinda's splendid cream teas with generous sized scones, jam and cream. There are cakes and other sweet delights aplenty, including mince and apple slice, rock cakes and real melt-in-the-mouth shortbread.

Scolfe's, *Boreham Street, near Hailsham, East Sussex, tel 01323 833296*
This friendly village tearoom and restaurant, in a 14th century Grade II listed building, has a most delightful ambience, with lovely wooden furnishings and beautiful table linen. There is an excellent range of savoury dishes on offer, from sandwiches, baked

potatoes and salads to more extensive meals such as Sunday roasts, thickly-sliced ham with organic egg and chips, and pies including Game Pie when in season and Scolfe's homemade Sea Pie, with white fish, prawns and egg in a white sauce topped with cheese-coated creamed potato. To follow there are full cream teas with fresh clotted cream and preserves, homemade cakes and a good variety of desserts which might include bread and butter pudding, apple pie, or apple and mixed berry crumble. There is a good range of teas including Lemon and Ginger, Tranquility and Camomile.

The Mock Turtle, *4 Pool Valley, Brighton, tel 01273 327380*
In the heart of this most cosmopolitan of South Coast resorts is a very traditional English tearoom where time seems to have stood still, from the pretty patterned wall paper and wooden tables to the willow pattern crockery and old-fashioned cash register. Even on weekdays, space is at a premium in its two tightly-packed dining areas, but any wait to be served is well worthwhile. The fare is traditional and wholesome; specials may include scotch gammon, back bacon or fillet of place or cod, and there is a choice of soups, omelettes and melt-in-the-mouth rarebits, done to perfection. To follow, there is a quite irresistible combination of warm scone with clotted cream and home-made lemon curd – truly, heaven on a plate – but if waistlines do not permit such excesses, there are anchovy and marmite toasts on offer as well as a variety of cakes.

St Martins Tea Rooms, *3 St Martins Street, Chichester, West Sussex, tel 01243 786715*
The interior of St Martins Tea Rooms is a delight, with its many nooks, roaring fires on cold days, exposed beams and brickwork, carpeting and wooden furniture. It is a deliciously cosy haven in winter, whilst in the heat of summer diners can enjoy the secluded brick and stone garden. The tearoom prides itself on its healthy organic food, with no tinned produce, artificial flavourings, colours or preservatives; it has won the Heartbeat Award for "exceptionally healthy food and cleanliness." Savoury fare includes lentil and vegetable soup, delicious Welsh rarebits, mushroom and cheese toasties, grilled vegetable cake and smoked salmon open sandwiches, while sweet treats include sultana scones, nutty flapjacks, chocolate cake, lemon sponge and really amazing moist banana bread.

***Shepherds, *35 Little London, Chichester, West Sussex, tel 01243 774761*
A regular recipient of Tea Council Awards of Excellence and three times Tea Council Top Tea Place Of the Year, Shepherds is arguably THE place to take tea in Sussex. It offers a good range of teas, including Pure Assam, Green Teas such as Gunpowder or Jasmine, and finest Darjeeling famous for its rich Muscatel flavour. Specials might include Greek-style feta cheese salad served with Mediterranean bread, open roast beef sandwich served with horseradish salad, or courgette and brie quiche with half a jacket potato. The savoury house specialities are the rarebits, including Welsh, buck, stilton

with tomato, bacon with mushroom, and brie with bacon; sandwiches include brie with cranberry and lettuce, BLT, and egg mayonnaise and cress; and there are jacket potatoes crammed with tuna mayonnaise or garlic mushrooms. The Shepherds Afternoon Tea provides a most English dining experience, with fluffy egg sandwiches, a huge fruit scone, jam and clotted cream, while summer fare includes a combination of cream tea with salmon sandwiches and a bowl of strawberries. Mouthwatering sweet things include orange or lemon slices, Mars Bar Crunch, iced ginger cake or magnificent roulade, arguably Shepherds' finest dessert choice.

Dolly's Pantry, *6-8 West Street, Ditchling, East Sussex, tel 01273 842708*
The word "cosy" might have been invented for this deliciously old-fashioned traditional village tearoom adjoining a bakery; particularly popular is the back room with its cluster of simple furnishings and large fireplace, while in the summer, diners can enjoy the garden. The sandwiches are quite simply magnificent, with generous slices of fresh bread accommodating a variety of sumptuous fillings including egg and bacon or beef and horseradish. Specials may include homemade quiche, macaroni cheese or cottage pie, while a dazzling variety of cakes on display in the bakery may range from chocolate muesli wedges to Viennese fingers. Or there is "Dolly's famous Cream Tea" consisting of 2 warm scones, one plain and one fruit, with clotted cream, strawberry jam, butter and house tea.

Robsons, *22A The High Street, Lewes, East Sussex, tel 01273 480654*
Near the bottom of the hill on the main street of the county town of East Sussex is this small and friendly tearoom. The room itself is light with lovely wooden seats and a big bay window looking out on to a very attractive enclosed mature hillside garden, and the food is of a uniformly high quality. What could be more English than its Sussex Cream Tea, consisting of cucumber sandwiches, fruit scone with butter, clotted cream and strawberry jam, and Sussex fruit cake. Savoury fare includes filled granary baps, croissants and foccaccia and ciabatta rolls, fillings including egg mayonnaise and a variety of meats, each served with coleslaw and deliciously moreish crisps. The little cheese scones are simply delectable, and there is a good variety of sweet temptations which might include shortbread, Rice Krispie cake and wild berry cheesecake.

Ye Olde Tea Shoppe, *North Street, Midhurst, West Sussex, tel 01730 817081*
While many tearooms offer a much-reduced menu towards the end of the afternoon, the owners of this popular and friendly establishment, once a sweet shop and for a while the home of the novelist H.G. Wells, pride themselves on offering a full menu until closing time every day of the week. Diners can choose between the front room, on two levels, a cosy parlour and a pretty garden. There are many teas to choose from including Apple & Cinnamon, Strawberry, Peppermint and Orange Passion; a range of hot snacks and sandwiches from bacon rarebit to jacket potato with salmon; a good

range of specials with a roast dish usually available on Sundays; and to finish, a splendid variety of sweet temptations including beautiful date slices, cakes, cheesecake (the ginger cheesecake is especially recommended) or crumble.

The Tea Tree,
12 High Street, Winchelsea, East Sussex, tel 01797 226102
The Tea Tree is a lovely tea room in a beautiful house on a quiet street in one of the prettiest small towns in Sussex. The décor is quite delightful, the low beams and wooden tables, topped with nice chequered tablecloths, enhancing the cottagey atmosphere. There is a wide choice of teas including not only staples such as Earl Grey, Darjeeling and Lapsang Souchong but more unusual brews such as the scented Friendship Tea flavoured with cinnamon. Hot specials might include smoked haddock fish pie, sausagemeat and apple plait or potato and broccoli bake with crusty bread, while the choice of sandwiches

Ye Olde Tea Shoppe at Midhurst, once the home of H.G. Wells, and now offering a wide range of appetising fare throughout the day.

includes really beautifully fluffy egg mayonnaise, tuna mayonnaise, and brie and bacon. To finish, there is home-made cake including quite exceptional iced ginger.

TOP TEN EYESORES IN SUSSEX

Beeding Cement Works on a wet day; the beautiful village of Steyning is just two miles distant.

Beeding Cement Works, *Upper Beeding, West Sussex*
Thousands of motorists use the A283 Bramber-Shoreham road as a convenient route to the sea from the north of the county and from Surrey. But pleasant thoughts of sun-kissed beaches are put on hold by the quite extraordinary conglomeration of old industrial buildings and units around the Beeding Cement Works. The buildings themselves, tall, ugly, gaunt and with neglect and dereliction written all over them, look like ghettoes in Moscow during the Cold War, while the units around them seem to have proliferated and generated huge amounts of rubbish, rubble and scrap, just yards from the lovely river bank of the Adur and the South Downs.

The Odeon and Brighton Centre, *King's Road, Brighton*
It is hard to say which of these two buildings, standing adjacent to each other on the Brighton seafront just yards from Palace Pier, is the uglier. The main body of the Brighton Centre is a severe grey, topped with a layer of stark red brick, and a big slab of white wrapped over the top right corner like an enormous piece of tissue. The Odeon's base is a ghastly grey brick, with one of the nastiest most uninviting central doorways imaginable; the middle part is faded yellow; and the roof has a design which was doubtless perceived at the time as exciting and futuristic but now just

Odeon and Brighton Centre.

looks appallingly naff. The whole is an affront to Brighton's Regency associations and heritage.

Edward Street *at its junction with John Street, Brighton*
Whilst Brighton boasts some of the finest Regency architecture in the country, and many wonderful things to see, there are some less appealing corners of the city and this is arguably the worst. From this junction can be seen the long tall masses of the law courts, the police station and the Job Centre, each unimaginatively designed, unyielding, unforgiving, grimly functional, unloved and unlovely. High blocks of flats are clearly visible behind, while an untidy assembly of pubs, cafes and houses lie on the other side of the road. If you want further punishment, continue a short way up Edward Street to the Spiritualist Church – ugly building, uninspiring setting.

Pontins, *Camber, East Sussex*
The sign outside it, "MOBILE TOP UP'S" sets the scene for this prison-camp-like construction, allegedly a place for enjoyment and leisure, that has been seemingly plonked down on the edge of a quiet village at the very south-eastern tip of Sussex, famous for its sands. The enormous blue and grey main building, which looks as though it might have been made out of pieces of Lego, seems wholly incongruous in this small seaside community. It is complemented by rows of dull brick chalets with red railings, while the barriers outside could easily serve to perpetuate the notion that this is some form of penal institution. Beach-lovers and holidaymakers deserve better.

Metro House, *Northgate, Chichester, West Sussex*
The walker travelling up through Chichester's main south-north thoroughfares, South Street and North Street, will enjoy some of the loveliest Georgian architecture in southern England. However a rude shock is in store at the end of North Street: straight ahead, on an island in the middle of a busy roundabout, is Metro House, a hideously ugly modern office block fronted by huge windows and with grey concrete sides, devoid of any architectural merit at all and a world away from Chichester's architectural treasures. Behind Metro House is a building that used to be a shoe-repair shop but it is now boarded up and looks scruffy and neglected.

Redbrick shelter, *Devil's Dyke, West Sussex*

Devil's Dyke is one of the loveliest spots in Sussex, with glorious views from the summit and superb walks along the top of the escarpment. It is a thousand pities, therefore, that the view from the ridge on which the triangulation point is built should be obscured by a redbrick shelter, which while not without its historical and curiosity value, has become something of a magnet for graffiti artists and looks wholly out of keeping with the beautiful unspoilt scenery on all sides. Were it to be removed, the resultant view from the ridge would surely be unparalleled not only in Sussex but in the whole of south-east England.

Lloyds TSB Building, *Durrington, Worthing, West Sussex*

Durrington is a pleasant leafy suburb of Worthing with many trim and attractive rows of houses and shops. However, towering above these buildings is the huge grey stone lump that is Lloyds TSB building, visible for miles around and devoid of any charm, chasisma or grandeur. The adjoining NHS building, a shapeless mass of brick, is scarcely lovlier.

***Central Peacehaven, *East Sussex*

Pevsner endorsed the views of many that Peacehaven was a rash on the countryside, going further and saying "there is no worse in England." In fact many parts of the village are trim, well cared for and no worse than many other modern developments on the south coast, but the central area bordering the A259, particularly between Roderick Avenue and Victoria Avenue, is a truly horrible mish mash of modern architectural styles, none remotely appealing to the eye, housing a mixture of residences and shops. In vain does one look for a building of the remotest historical or architectural interest. Arguably the prize for the worst should go to the shapeless Channel View, a long building with a domestic appliance show room on ground level and a great red-brick lump above it containing flats, but there are many other candidates for awards for awfulness.

Marine Court, *St Leonards, East Sussex*

This enormous block of flats and shops looking out on to the seafront, built in 1937/38, was designed to look like an ocean-going liner. But while the original intention may have been to create something imposing and majestic, befitting

Marine Court, St Leonards.

a high-class Sussex resort, the building is in fact a monstrosity, described by Pevsner as "the first modernistic affront to the English seaside." The ground floor consists of a nondescript row of shops and other commercial premises, while the flats above are crammed into a huge, stark, severe fading white block totally devoid of architectural merit, and looking wholly incongruous in the context of the buildings on either side.

Teville Gate, *Worthing, West Sussex*
Worthing's image as a genteel and neat South Coast resort is rudely dispelled by the mess of buildings and premises that lie between the station and Chapel Road, one of the town's principal shopping areas. This mess, known as Teville Gate, is dominated by an enormous ugly multi-storey car park, but its more infamous horrors have been in the form of a parade of shops which fell into spectacular decay and were natural targets for crime and vandalism. Many of these shops have now been demolished, but some remain and the whole area – for many, their first sight of Worthing – exudes neglect, decay and charmlessness.

TOP TEN GREAT CHURCHES IN SUSSEX

Arundel Cathedral, *Arundel, West Sussex*
The cathedral was designed in 1868/9 by the 15th Duke of Norfolk and built between 1870 and 1875. It is a vast building, characterised by its very tall narrow aisles, and because it is situated at the highest point in the town, it stands out magnificently when the town is viewed from a distance. Built in the French Gothic style of the early 14th century, it was intended to be even bigger: there were originally plans for a north-west tower but it was never built. Pevsner states that "The feeling of *ecclesia triumphans* which Catholics during those years must have had could not have found a more elated expression." Inside, the piers – the walls separating the nave from the side aisles – are of great height, creating a most impressive effect, although the interior boasts no other outstanding features.

St Mary & St Blaise, *Boxgrove, Chichester, West Sussex*

The west door of Arundel's Roman Catholic Cathedral, built in Gothic style in the late 19th century.

The Priory Church of Boxgrove was founded from Normandy in 1117, and indeed the present church's exterior looks very French with steeply pitched roofs, flying buttresses and pyramidical tower cap. The present church is surrounded by former monastic buildings, with remnants of the original nave and priory buildings lying to the west and north. The present nave was the chancel of the original and was built in the early 13th century. The two outstanding features of the present building are the rib vaulting, decorated with early 16th century painting of Rococo floral pattern including Tudor roses and de la Warre heraldry, and the de la Warre chantry of 1532 with pure Gothic architecture and magnificent carvings of both Gothic and classical origin. The reredos is the work of George Gilbert Scott.

St Bartholomew's, *Ann Street, Brighton*
This church was built between 1872 and 1874 and designed by Father Arthur Wagner. Its huge interior boasts the highest nave of any parish church in England, rising 135ft from the floor, and with no chancel there is a huge sense of space; Simon Jenkins comments that the roof, linked to the floor by walls of unadorned brick, "seems lost in the clouds." The sanctuary, designed in 1895, is described as a "masterpiece" of the designer Henry Wilson; there is an Art Nouveau altar rail of brass with blue enamel insets, and behind is a dazzling mosaic mural; and the font and pulpit are made of green marble.

St Michael's, *Victoria Road, Brighton*
This church was built over 30 years in the 19th century by two masters of Victorian architecture, Bodley and Burges. The jewel of Bodley's part of the church is the Lady Chapel with its chequerboard floor, white panelled ceiling and delicate reredos, while windows include Burne-Jones' "superb" depiction of the Flight Into Egypt. Burges' part is described by Simon Jenkins as "spectacular," with massive Gothic arcades and three huge lancets lighting the chancel. A feature of particular interest is Nicholls' misericords with such delights as boxing frogs and a grasshopper riding a snail.

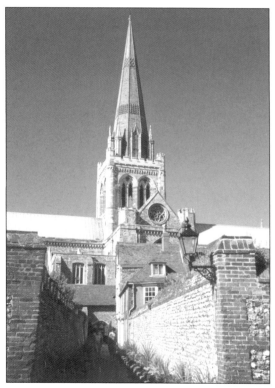

Arguably the most famous landmark in Sussex, Chichester Cathedral; its spire replaces the one that was destroyed in 1861.

***Chichester Cathedral, *Chichester, West Sussex*

Unquestionably the greatest church building in Sussex. The exterior and interior of the cathedral, which dates back to the end of the 11th century, are equally impressive. The cathedral's lofty spire, rebuilt following the destruction of the previous spire in a storm in 1861, can be seen from the tops of the South Downs many miles away, and dominates the surrounding landscape. Seen from close up, particularly in the tranquil Canon Lane to the south, it assumes an awesome grandeur. Highlights of the interior include Norman sculptures, the magnificent fourteenth century choirstalls, the imposing fifteenth century Arundel Screen, the shrine of St Richard of Chichester, John Piper's altar tapestry and Marc Chagall's stained glass window depicting Psalm 150. There is a separate belltower which is thought to date from around 1428, and contains a ring of eight bells, the earliest dated 1583.

Lancing College Chapel, *Lancing, West Sussex*
This massive building, with an external height of 150 ft, is visible for miles around, and as you enter it you are immediately struck by its sheer vastness. With an internal height

of 94ft it is the fourth highest church interior in England. Its foundation stone was laid in 1868, 20 years after the foundation of Lancing College itself by Nathaniel Woodard to whom the chapel is a testament. The style of the chapel is early 14th century English Gothic, with 13th century French influences. Its outstanding features are its painted ceiling, the comparatively recent (1978) stained glass Rose Window at its west end, and the massive tapestries above the High Altar, woven in 1933 and at one time the biggest in the country.

St Mary's, *Shoreham-by-Sea, West Sussex*
The full name of this church is St Mary de Haura, literally "of the harbour," and indeed this church was begun by the Normans in 1130 to serve the harbour that was to replace the one at Old Shoreham, a victim of silting. Nearly 900 years later, the tower still dominates the town, the harbour and the beach. The crossing and transepts of 1130 still survive, as do the upper tower, begun in about 1180 and described by Simon Jenkins as a "textbook of comparative 12th century style." The glory of St Mary's, also dating from the 12th century, is the choir interior: each side displays strongly contrasting motifs, the north arcade late Norman and the south arcade early Gothic.

St Mary's, *Sompting, Worthing, West Sussex*
This church boasts England's finest Saxon steeple, built early in the 11th century, although the foundations can be traced back to 960. Each side of the tower ends in a steep gable, and the roof is made up of 4 diamond shaped surfaces meeting in a point; it is known as Rhenish helm, and is unique in England. The carvings on the arches of the tower interior, believed to date back as early as the steeple, are among the earliest examples of English architectural carving. The church retains not only Saxon carving but Saxon sculpture too; one clearly discernible figure is that of an abbot with a book propped up beside him. The rest of the church is mostly late Norman. A north transept and southern chamber were both added by the Knights Templar to whom the church was donated near the end of the 12th century, and the church has a font which has been in use since Norman times.

St Andrew's, *Steyning, West Sussex*
Described by Simon Jenkins as a "bruiser of a building," this church was given by Edward the Confessor to the Norman monks who demolished the Saxon church that previously stood here, and built another church of which a substantial part remains today. This includes the tremendous nave, chancel arch, and nave arcades and clerestories which had all been finished by the end of the 12th century. The arcades and clerestories are decorated with quite magnificent Norman carvings depicting the heads of both humans and animals, and other features include dogtooth, scallops and stone zigzags. In the 16th century was added the west tower and the reredos of 48 carved panels, one of which bears the coat of arms of Henry VIII. In the porch there

is a broken coffin lid that was taken from the Saxon burial ground; it is possible that it might have come from the grave of St Cuthman whose resting place is here.

St Thomas', *Winchelsea, East Sussex*

The original church was built under the patronage of Edward I. The present church, which dates back to the early 14th century, boasts a formidable interior, and Simon Jenkins comments that the piscina and sedilia might be those of a cathedral. The chief glory of the church, however, is the collection of medieval tombs which line the walls of both aisles. On the north wall are splendid depictions of a knight and lady and gentleman of black Sussex marble, with lavishly decorated canopies. Opposite, in the south aisle, are two altared tombs reputedly being those of two Wardens of the Cinque Ports in prayer, with magnificent carved representations of lion and angels. The church also boasts an unusual set of windows, created in the 1930's as a memorial to the Great War with the theme of the elements of earth, fire and water.

TOP TEN HOUSES IN SUSSEX

Charleston,
near Lewes, East Sussex,
tel 01323 811265

Charleston is a 16th century unpretentious house which was modernised around 1800. In 1916 it became the home of Vanessa Bell who was the artist sister of Virginia Woolf, her husband the art critic Clive Bell, and her lover Duncan Grant. Vanessa Bell and Duncan Grant painted the tables,

Charleston Farmhouse.

bedheads, cupboards, walls and chairs with abstract patterns and naturalistic designs, while the interior is described by Keith Spence as having "an endearing and muddled amateurishness about it." The dining room contains black stencilled wallpaper and a large portrait of Lytton Strachey on the wall; in the bathroom, even the sides of the bath are painted; every inch of Duncan's bedroom is painted; and the studio is left as it was when painting ceased here in the 1970's.

Firle Place, *near Lewes, East Sussex, tel 01273 858335*

This house, built in Tudor times by Sir John Gage, sits very picturesquely in the shade of the South Downs and is noteworthy for its extensive art collections. In the early 18th century it was very substantially altered and added to by one of Sir John's descendants, Sir William Gage. Particular features of note include the downstairs drawing room, described by Simon Jenkins as a "dazzling array of 'Ionian white and gold;'" the impressively-sized Great Hall dominated by a flamboyant van Dyck; the Little Hall containing the Great Staircase, with its cheerful white and pale blue plasterwork; the downstairs dining room with beautiful Dutch landscape paintings; the upstairs drawing room with its Chippendale cabinets; and the Long Gallery with paintings by Reynolds, Hoppner, Mengs and Teniers.

Glynde Place, *near Lewes, East Sussex, tel 01273 858224*

This is a magnificent Elizabethan manor house with a beautiful Downland setting. It was built by an ironmaster named William Morley from local flint and stone from Normandy, and there were substantial additions in the 18th century. There is fine collection of paintings, furniture, silver and embroidery, while paintings include work

Glynde Place.

by Brueghel, Lely, Guardi and Canaletto. The house's showpiece is the upstairs gallery with dark panelling that includes woodcarving in the style of Gibbons.

Goodwood House, *near Chichester, West Sussex, tel 01243 755000*

The first building on the site was erected in the 17th century as a hunting lodge; wings were added to it in the 18th century and it was further extended between 1800 and 1806. It is noteworthy for its magnificent art collection including works by Stubbs, Romney, Ramsay, Mengs, Lely and van Dyck. Among the best rooms are the front hall with a fine collection of Stubbs' paintings, the music room with its fireplace by William Kent, and the wonderfully restored Egyptian dining room with furniture of mahogany and ebony.

***Parham House, *Storrington, West Sussex, tel 01903 744888*

Parham was begun in 1577 by Thomas Palmer. The house's interiors are mostly of the late 16th and early 17th centuries. The Great Hall has a ceiling with heavy pendants and huge windows; the adjacent parlour boasts a lovely set of portraits by John Fawcett, manager of Covent Garden Theatre; the Great Chamber and West Room both have magnificent flame-stitch embroidery; the ante-room has an exquisite Coromandel cabinet and walls of Hungarian needlework; the Green Room is dedicated to the spirit of discovery of the 18th century with globes, prints of yachts and Reynolds' painting Portrait of Omai; and on the 2nd floor is the long gallery, with beautiful views out to the South Downs and some more fantastic embroidery. Indeed the house has the best collection of historic needlework outside London. Simon Jenkins writes "Nothing at Parham is superfluous, nothing unloved. It is a place of magic."

Petworth House, *Petworth, West Sussex, tel 01798 342207*
Though the house, with its French chateau-like exterior, dates back more than 6 centuries, little of the original work remains apart from the chapel. Wholesale rebuilding took place between 1688 and 1696 by Charles Seymour, 6th Duke of Somerset, and the reconstruction was completed by the Duke's descendant, the 2nd Earl of Egremont. Today it is noteworthy for a magnificent collection of paintings with works by Turner, Rembrandt, Holbein, Gainsborough and van Dyck. Of particular interest is the Grinling Gibbons Room with many superb examples of Gibbons' amazingly intricate carvings. Other highlights are the Marble Hall, Grand Staircase, Turner Room, Sculpture Gallery and chapel which contains remarkable woodwork.

Royal Pavilion, *Brighton, tel 01273 290900*
In 1815 the Prince Regent appointed John Nash to build a palace to effectively replace the simple Marine Pavilion by Henry Holland, and the Royal Pavilion was the result. It was completed in 1823 and remains the most striking and stunning building in Brighton and arguably in Sussex. Decorated in Chinese taste with an Indian exterior consisting of onion domes and minarets, it is as breathtaking on the inside as outside; highlights include the Banqueting Room, a riot of Chinese dragons and huge chandeliers, the Saloon with its domed ceiling painted as a sky lightly covered with cloud, and the Music Room with walls decorated with Chinese landscapes and giant chandelier which, to quote Simon Jenkins, "drips like a lotus flower in a sea of gold."

St Mary's House, *Bramber, Steyning, West Sussex, tel 01903 816205*
This enchanting house with its superb black and white exterior, dating back to approximately 1470, is still a lived-in home. Described as a house of "fascination and mystery," it boasts a number of fine rooms, including the Monk's Parlour, notable for its huge "dragon" beam and 17th century inglenook; the Hall, embellished with beautiful 17th century gilded wall-leather; the Octagonal Dining Room displaying over 80 costume dolls; the Painted Room, with its fascinating "trompe l'oeil" murals said to have been painted for a visit by Elizabeth I; and the Library, containing a unique private collection of works by the Victorian comic poet Thomas Hood.

The magnificent timber-framed St Mary's House at Bramber, built in the 15th century.

Standen, *near East Grinstead, West Sussex, tel 01342 323029*
Built in 1891 by the Arts and Crafts architect, Philip Webb, and now owned by the National Trust, Standen's exterior is an extraordinary mix of styles, with a Queen Anne entrance, a gabled garden front, and stone, pebbledash, brick and weatherboarding everywhere. There is magnificent furniture with most of the fabrics, wallpaper and tiles from the Morris firm; the drawing room is blessed with particularly rich wallpapers and hangings and there are Morris "Tulip and Rose" curtains by the fireplace. There is a conservatory filled with bougainvillaea, plumbago and oleander, and the terracing is thick with rhododendrons and azaleas.

Uppark, *near South Harting, West Sussex, tel 01730 825415*
This is a replica of a 17th century mansion that was burnt down in 1989, and it has been restored to look just as it did before the fire. It has an immaculate exterior, with nine bays of lofty windows, dressed in stone on redbrick, rising to a hipped roof. Open to visitors on the ground floor is the Dining Room with its endlessly reflecting mirrors, the double-cube Saloon, decorated in greyish-white and gold with Batoni portraits and an Adamish Rococo plasterwork ceiling, and the Red Drawing Room with its Chippendale furniture. There is a complete set of servants' quarters below stairs, and the Stewards' Hall, where the upper servants would have dined, boasts a superb dolls' house.

TOP TEN NATURAL COASTAL WONDERS IN SUSSEX

Beachy Head.

***Beachy Head, *near Eastbourne, East Sussex*

Undoubtedly the most famous coastal feature in Sussex, the clifftop of Beachy Head stands a staggering 535ft above the sea below, with tremendous views in all directions (see Top Ten Viewpoints in Sussex). Those with a head for heights can make for the edge of the sheer cliffs, and view the 125ft high lighthouse, about a century old. Believed to derive from the French "beau chef," meaning "beautiful headland," Beachy Head is a mecca for butterfly hunters, with 20 of the 50 or so species of butterfly having been seen here including cabbage whites, Adonis blues and dark green fritillaries. Since 1990 it has become once more a breeding ground for falcons, and it is one of the best places in Sussex to see the stone curlew. Other birds that might be seen here are the dark grey-winged herring gull, jackdaw, rook, fulmar, rock pipit, guillemot, tern, crag martin, chaffinch, bullfinch, fieldfare, collar dove, greater and lesser black-backed gull, lapwing, linnet, pied wagtail, owl, starling, swift and greater-spotted woodpecker; on the ground you may see a fox, slow worm, badger, common lizard, grass snake, hedgehog, mole, vole or shrew, while plants include bellflower, scabious and pink centaury.

Camber and Broomhill Sands, *near Rye, East Sussex*

The tremendously varied coastal scenery of Sussex has at its eastern extremity a carpet of golden sands, Camber Sands being the name for the area of beach immediately adjacent to the village of Camber; walking eastwards from Camber Sands you will imperceptibly find yourself on Broomhill Sands! Together they form one of the best and most popular stretches of beach on the entire coastline of Southern England. The superb expanse of gently-ridged golden sand, which stretches out to sea for half a mile or more at low tide, is complemented by extensive sand dunes along the back of the beach. Among the dunes, marram grass has been planted by the Forestry Commission to preserve the special qualities of the sands from the effects of the wind. There are lovely views from Camber Sands back towards the cliffs round Fairlight, and to the beautiful old town of Rye.

Climping Beach, *near Littlehampton, West Sussex*

This is unusual among Sussex beaches as having a rural, totally unspoilt setting with none of the "seaside resort" trappings apart from perhaps the odd ice cream van; access is along a narrow road from the A259, and on either side of the access road there is open countryside. From the top of the shingle there are glorious views to Arundel Castle and Cathedral as well as the South Downs. The sea hereabouts may yield cockles, whelks, shrimps and cuttlefish; there are splendid sands to be enjoyed at low tide; from the dunes a little to the east of the access road can be seen many birds including kestrel, ringed plover and oystercatcher; and plants within the dunes might include sea kale and birds' foot trefoil.

Cuckmere Haven, *near Seaford, East Sussex*

Cuckmere Haven is the valley between Seaford Head and the Seven Sisters where the Cuckmere River reaches the sea; although a new, straight cut was created in the mid-19th century, the course of the old river is evident in its spectacular meanders through the valley from the A259 to the English Channel. The valley, and the river mouth itself, is totally unspoilt with no buildings or port complex at all, and it is the only river valley in Sussex to provide a natural merging of meadow marsh, saltings and a wild seashore. There are plenty of well-signposted walks and magnificent views to the surrounding cliffs.

East Head, *West Wittering, West Sussex*

This is a huge spit of sand, both dunes and harder sand, which has been formed and shaped by the surrounding seas. In 1966 it was taken over by the National Trust and as well as a superbly unspoilt area of sand for walking and relaxing, extremely popular with visitors at all times of the year, it is an important area for birds and plants. Feathered visitors include the lapwing, snipe and black-tailed godwit, whilst among the dunes can be found marram grass and glasswort. On a clear day the views from the end of the spit are tremendous, with vistas stretching as far afield as the South Downs and the Isle of Wight.

Hastings to Fairlight, *East Sussex*
Between Hastings and Fairlight Cove lie 5 miles of magnificent unspoilt scenery with deep wooded glens, heather clad hills and fine sandstone cliffs consisting of some of the oldest rocks in the South East. Over 540 acres were formed into the so-called Hastings Country Park in 1974. Highlights include Ecclesbourne Glen, a wooded valley that is ideal nesting territory for tits and warblers; Fairlight Glen, carpeted in spring with bluebells and wood anemones; Lovers Seat, a tremendous viewpoint beside which is a Sarsen stone; Warren Glen, the slopes above which are coated with oak, hazel, beech, ash and golden saxifrage; and Firehills, an area of beautiful heathland, its name derived from the bright fiery colour of the gorse-covered slopes in summer.

Longmere Point, *Thorney Island, West Sussex*
Longmere Point is at the far south-eastern tip of Thorney Island, on the edge of Chichester Harbour, and offers tremendous views in all directions. Inland are the fine wooded hills round Kingley Vale, while out to sea you can admire the Manhood peninsula and the great sand spit of East Head. Immediately before you is Pilsey Island with a tremendous array of bird life, and from Longmere Point you might look out for wild swans, brent geese, shelducks, curlews, red-breasted mergansers, black-headed gulls, dunlins, sandwich terns, ringed plovers, oystercatchers and redshanks.

Seaford Head and Hope Gap, *near Seaford, East Sussex*
An impressive clifftop with tremendous views both westwards to Brighton and beyond, and eastwards to the Seven Sisters, Seaford Head is the site of a triangular Iron Age hillfort and today is a nature reserve boasting 308 acres which comprise not only downland but mudflats and meadowland; it is home to 250 species of plants and a large amount of wildfowl. An eastward descent of the cliff brings you to Hope Gap, a delightfully secluded spot in a valley between rising cliffs. A detour down a flight of steps takes you to the rocky pavements separating the cliffs from the sea.

Hope Gap.

Selsey Bill, *Selsey, West Sussex*

The southernmost point of Sussex, Selsey Bill is a tremendous place to stand and watch the sea; if you are brave enough, the best time is when this most exposed spot on the whole of the Sussex coastline is being lashed by waves at the height of a storm. On a clear day you can contrast the two completely different views obtained by looking north-westwards back towards Medmerry and Bracklesham, and north-eastwards towards Bognor Regis with a backcloth of the Sussex Downs.

Seven Sisters, *between Seaford and Eastbourne, East Sussex*

The Seven Sisters are seven spectacular chalk cliffs forming the eastern extreme of the South Downs, and owe their origin to geological activity between 50 and 100 million years ago. Each clifftop or "sister" has a name; the depressions separating each clifftop are the valleys of ancient rivers. The unspoilt chalk hills attract many birds including the fulmar, wheatear and jackdaw, plants that include round-headed rampion, carline thistle and certain fungi, and also butterflies including the blue butterfly, red admiral and clouded yellow. At the eastern end of the Seven Sisters is a freak cleft in the South Downs known as Birling Gap.

Seaford Head

TOP TEN FAMILY DAYS OUT IN SUSSEX

A day out in and around Ashdown Forest:

This handsome weatherboarded house in Hartfield is THE place for Winnie-the-Pooh fans everywhere.

The principal attraction of the day is the Ashdown Forest Llama Park (tel 01825 712040), one of the leading llama breeding centres in the country. The park enjoys unrivalled views over the forest and as you take a leisurely stroll round the farm walk you will encounter over 100 llama and alpaca characters. The park museum enables you to learn more about llamas and alpacas and their domestication in South America over 5000 years ago, the South American Craft Shop has a wide range of craft goods and lots of "llamarabilia," and the Alpaca Shop stocks an inspirational range of designer alpaca knitwear. There is also a coffee shop and picnic area. From here, take a leisurely drive through the forest to Hartfield and its shop Pooh Corner (tel 01892 770456) which has the largest selection of Winnie The Pooh merchandise to be found anywhere in the world! By driving back to East Grinstead, just north-west of the forest, and proceeding a few miles beyond the town to Turners Hill, you could round off the day with a trip to Tulleys Farm (01342 717071) which besides farm animals offers a huge variety of amusements for children and numerous special events throughout the year. The farm has an award-winning farm shop and tea room.

The Bluebell Railway, *near Haywards Heath, West Sussex, tel 01825 720800*
The Bluebell Railway is a preserved all-steam railway between Sheffield Park and Kingscote, part of the old Lewes to East Grinstead railway line. You do not have to be

a railway buff to enjoy the experience of travelling in steam locomotives through beautiful Sussex countryside. Over 30 locomotives are on display plus Victorian, 1930's and 1950's stations, while Sheffield Park, the southern terminus of the preserved line, has locomotive sheds, a restaurant, museum, shop and model railway. A Pullman dining service is often available on Saturday evenings and Sunday lunchtimes. Nearby are the famous Sheffield Park Gardens (see Top Ten Gardens in Sussex). A few miles to the north of the railway terminus and gardens is Heaven Farm (tel 01825 790226), a 600 year old unique farm including parkland, ponds, wallabies, Sussex Rural Life Museum and the Bluebell nature trail. There is also an excellent tea room.

***A day out in Brighton

The chief glory of Brighton is the Royal Pavilion (See Top Ten Houses in Sussex), the former seaside residence of King George IV and one of the most exotically beautiful buildings in the British Isles. Perhaps of greater appeal to children is the city's Sea Life Centre (tel 01273 604234) with spectacular marine displays in what is the world's oldest functioning aquarium. Visitors can see 100 species in their natural habitat including seahorses, sharks and rays, and a large number of exhibitions including Adventures At 20,000 Leagues, a NASA-designed observation tunnel and a Captain Pugwash Quiz Trail. Brighton, with its flourishing Palace Pier, golden sands, excellent bathing, famous Volks Electric Railway, bustling marina with a vast number of shops and restaurants, and variety of museums and galleries, is a hugely popular place to

Royal Pavilion, Brighton.

enjoy the seaside, while the needs of shopaholics are catered for by the smart modern Churchill Square shopping complex, and the narrow streets of more specialist and expensive shops known as the Lanes; there are around 700 independent shops in the city. Brighton boasts many superb examples of Regency architecture, especially in the area around Regency Square.

A day with the Seven Sisters

The Seven Sisters are seven magnificent chalk cliffs between Seaford and Eastbourne (see Top Ten Natural Coastal Wonders in Sussex) offering beautiful clifftop walking. Close to Birling Gap, at the eastern end of the cliffs, is the Seven Sisters Sheep Centre (tel 01323 423302), a family-run farm for animal lovers of all ages, and voted Best Family Attraction In Sussex. The centre contains the world's largest collection of breeds of sheep, and there are many other farm animals, tame enough to touch and feed. Springtime visitors can enjoy seeing the newborn lambs, while summer visitors will see the sheep being sheared and milked. There are tractor rides for children and the centre has a tea room and gift shop. From the centre it is a short drive to the totally unspoilt Cuckmere Haven (see Top Ten Natural Coastal Wonders in Sussex) where there is a popular pub in the Golden Galleon, and an excellent visitor information centre at Exceat Bridge.

A day out in Eastbourne

There truly is something for everybody in Eastbourne, one of the most elegant seaside towns in Sussex. Shopaholics will enjoy the excellent shopping centre and its many intriguing side streets of antique and junk shops. Horticulture enthusiasts will love the banks of flowers adorning many of the streets and the delightful gardens including the well-known Carpet Gardens which have been established in the town for more than a century. Insect-lovers will not want to miss the Butterfly Centre where they may watch for exotic butterflies and moths amongst jacaranda, hibiscus and bougainvillaea.

Culture buffs will head for the Towner Art Gallery and Local History Museum, while historians will want to see the Coastal Defence Museum in the Wish Tower and the redbrick fortress known as the Redoubt which also houses a museum. Lovers of the seaside can enjoy the beautiful sands or relax to music at the seafront bandstand, while children of all ages can take a

Fort Fun, Eastbourne.

ride on the seafront Dotto train, visit the 2-acre family fun park called Fort Fun (tel 01323 642833) and inspect the coal-fired miniature steam locomotives in the Miniature Steam Railway Adventure Park (tel 01323 520229). Further information on Eastbourne's principal attractions can be obtained by contacting 0906 711 2212.

A day out in Hastings

A town of immense historic interest in its own right, Hastings has a number of splendid attractions for the family. At Smugglers Adventure at St Clement's Caves, you can discover smugglers at work in the eerie caverns and passages of the caves; there is an interactive museum zone giving a hands-on opportunity to learn about Sussex smugglers, with exciting sound and light shows bringing the story to life. Underwater World provides the opportunity to explore the vibrant world within our oceans, perhaps the most interesting aspect of the exhibition being the sea-horse conservation corner. In White Rock Gardens is Clambers, a really splendid indoor and outdoor play centre for children up to 12 years old with a huge range of activities on offer. A trip to Hastings would not be complete without visiting the remains of the Norman castle and learning more about its intriguing past. There are tremendous walks on to the cliffs from Hastings towards Fairlight, and there are good beaches as well as all the traditional trappings of a seaside resort. Further information on Hastings' principal attractions is available on 01424 781111.

Drusillas Park, *Alfriston, East Sussex, tel 01323 874100*

Described as the best small zoo in the United Kingdom, Drusillas has a large variety of animals in naturalistic environments including meerkats, a walk-through bat enclosure, Penguin Bay, llama paddock, "Millennium Bugs," Petworld, and, new for 2005, Lar Gibbons. There is a huge amount for children to do, and special attractions for them within the complex include Monkey Kingdom, Treetops Lookout, Safari

Flyer, Penguin Plunge, Zoolympics Challenge and Explorers Lagoon, as well as an extensive play area. Throughout the year there are special events and displays which in 2005 included a Sheepdog Display, Creepy Crawlies Days and Reptile Weekends. A visit to Drusillas could be coupled with a trip to the beautiful nearby village of Alfriston (see Top Ten Historic Villages in Sussex).

Drusillas Park, Alfriston.

Fishers Farm Park, *Wisborough Green, West Sussex, tel 01403 700063*
Winner of the Farm Attraction Of The Year 2004, this is described as an "all-weather, all-inclusive great family day out," with a unique mixture of farmyard and dynamic adventure play. Farmyard animals include big horses, pigs, goats and lambs, as well as small animals such as rabbits and guinea pigs, and there is a pond with geese and ducks. Daily events include tractor, carousel and pony rides, shows in the air-conditioned theatre, bumper boats, quads, climbing wall and trampolines; there is an outdoor adventure park, large sandpit with diggers, a big paddling pool with a "beach area" around it, and indoor mini-gyms for smaller children. The park has a large indoor restaurant. A visit to Fishers Farm could be coupled with a more sedate stroll round Petworth, a few miles to the west, with its magnificent house and cottage museum (see Top Ten Historic Towns in Sussex).

Middle Farm, *Lewes, East Sussex, tel 01323 811411*
This is a working family farm at the foot of the South Downs. Visitors can see the farm's Jersey cows being milked and can also view pigs, sheep, chickens, ducks, donkeys and Banjo the shire horse. Children will love playing in the hay barn and admiring the baby calves, while adults will enjoy the famous Farm Shop with its fine range of country produce, local meat from the farm's own butchery, over 50 English cheeses and farmhouse baking. There is also a National Collection of Cider and Perry which stocks over 300 ciders, perries, wines, meads, liqueurs and apple juices, and there is an excellent

Middle Farm near Lewes, with its wide range of animals from baby chicks to shire horses, is a wonderful experience for children.

restaurant, gift shop and plant centre. A few miles to the north, near Halland, is the Bentley Wildfowl and Motor Museum (01825 840573). Here, hundreds of ducks, swans and geese from across the world can be seen on lakes and ponds along with flamingoes and peacocks. The motor museum boasts a fine array of veteran, Edwardian and vintage vehicles, while outside there are woodland walks and adventure playground.

The Observatory Science Centre, *Herstmonceux, East Sussex, tel 01323 832741*
With its domes and telescopes, the Science Centre is part of the former home of the Royal Greenwich Observatory and is one of the country's leading Science Centres with more than 100 exciting interactive exhibits. Visitors will be able to see heat, create clouds, touch a tornado, defy gravity, generate electricity, balance a beach ball on air and even become a ghost! There is a separate exhibition devoted to the story of the Royal Observatory, describing what the astronomers did at Greenwich and Herstmonceux, the huge telescopes they used and the discoveries they made. There is an outdoor science park called the Discovery Park with ingenious children's play activities, and within the complex there is a café and a shop which sells science toys as well as gifts, books and souvenirs. Throughout the year there are special events and activities on science and astronomy. A visit to the Centre could be coupled with a visit to Herstmonceux Castle which is immediately adjacent to the Science Centre (see Top Ten Castles in Sussex).

TOP TEN MUSEUMS/ EXHIBITIONS IN SUSSEX

Amberley Working Museum, *Amberley, Arundel, West Sussex, tel 01798 831370*
This is a 36-acre open-air museum that is dedicated to the industrial heritage of South East England. There are traditional craftspeople on site, including blacksmith, woodturner, broom-maker, foundry man, walking-stick maker, claypipe maker wheelwright and potter; there are stationary engines; there is a working narrow-gauge railway and a vintage bus collection, and the opportunity actually to travel on one of the buses to enable you to make your way round the site; and there is a print workshop, Connected Earth telecommunications display and EDF Electricity hall. The visitor can also enjoy the museum's nature trails, and there is a restaurant on site.

Battle Abbey and 1066 Battlefield, *Battle, East Sussex, tel 01424 773792*
By visiting this complex you will be able to relive one of the most famous days in England's history, the Battle of Hastings. Within the complex you will be able to enjoy an inclusive interactive audio tour of the 1066 battlefield and abbey, led by three characters who were witnesses to the day's events: a Saxon soldier, a Norman knight, and King Harold's mistress! There is a museum dedicated to abbey life which also includes a "Prelude to Battle" exhibition. Throughout the year there are colourful special events including the Battle Proms Concerts.

Buckleys Yesterday's World, *Battle, East Sussex, tel 01424 775378*
This museum enables you to step into the world of yesteryear and discover a "magical

Yesterday's World at Battle, with its celebration of life in bygone years, won the 2002 national Visitor Attraction Of The Year award.

story of shops and social history." You will be able to experience the evocative sights, sounds and smells in over thirty room and shop settings, authentically displayed in a medieval hall house. Displays include cobbled streets of a bygone age, a 1930's grocers, a chemist, a toyshop and Mrs Bumble's chocolate shop. You can smell the culinary delights of a Edwardian kitchen, peer into a maid's bedroom and children's nursery, and come face to face with Queen Victoria in her Throne Room where her nightdress and silk stockings, along with other royalty items, are on display. In the grounds there is an English country garden, a 1930's railway station, and bygone photographer's and cycle shops. There is an excellent gift shop too.

Fishbourne Roman Palace, *near Chichester, West Sussex, tel 01243 785859*
In 1960 a workman unwittingly discovered the remains of the largest Roman domestic building yet found north of the Alps. This led to extensive excavations revealing the remnant of a palatial building, possibly the home of a local king. The remains contained the largest and earliest group of in-situ Roman mosaic floors ever seen in Britain. Today's visitors will see the remains of the north wing of the palace inside a protecting building, and can view the superb mosaic floors, as well as the most significant finds from the many excavations, ranging from the personal to the exotic. The items are displayed with text, illustrations and models to relate the story of the site, and there is an introductory audio-visual programme. Surviving traces of the original formal palace gardens can also be seen, the formal garden being replanted to the original plan, and there is a small museum of Roman gardens. Refreshments are available.

How We Lived Then Museum Of Shops, *Eastbourne, East Sussex, tel 01323 737143*
This is one of the most comprehensive collections of its kind in the country, containing over 100,000 exhibits, and shops and other establishments made to look exactly as they were in bygone days. These include Mr Barton's grocery store, with biscuits being sold from glass-topped tins and nostalgic products such as Monkey-brand soap; an old seafarer's inn called the Admiral Lord Nelson where you will meet a sailor home on leave enjoying his pint, and you can inspect a collection of objects connected with Nelson; the wartime kitchen/living room complete with air raid shelter under the stairs; an Edwardian kitchen, staffed by housekeeper, cook and scullery maid; the ironmonger, selling everything from pot-menders to mouse traps; the music shop with its street organs and gramophones; and the toy shop with dolls, model trains and games. There is a well-stocked gift shop too.

Museum of Sussex Archaeology, *Lewes, East Sussex, tel 01273 486290*
The museum is housed in Barbican House, a large town house adjoining Lewes Castle. There are rooms devoted to the Stone Age and Bronze Age, the Romans and the Anglo-Saxons. Of special interest is the superb pre-Christian Saxon jewellery, and

there is a good collection of Saxon and Roman coins as well as some delightful bronze boars and Sussex pottery. The museum also houses an interactive touch-screen display called A Touch of Lewes and there is a sound and light show, The Story of Lewes Town. Just ten minutes away, on Southover High Street, is Anne of Cleves House, a traditional 15th century Wealden hall-house which includes a gallery that holds an important collection of Sussex ironwork. It is possible to buy a combined ticket to enable you to visit both properties as well as Lewes Castle.

Newhaven Fort, *Newhaven, East Sussex, tel 01273 517622*
This museum allows you the opportunity to step back into wartime Britain. The sights, sounds and even the smells of the two World Wars are to be found in a range of displays, audio-visual presentations and exhibits set inside a fortification where the massive walls, ramparts, gun emplacements and tunnels can still be seen. The museum itself is housed inside casemates which once served as living quarters for the soldiers stationed there. The World War I exhibition includes a video setting out the historical background to the conflict, and a recreated trench along the Western Front at the time of the Battle of the Somme in 1916; the World War II exhibition includes a "blitzed" home, an air raid shelter, a wartime kitchen, a brand new living memory display, and radio recordings of the period. There are many special events every year, and refreshments are available.

Paradise Park, Newhaven, *East Sussex, tel 01273 512123*
The park contains a number of attractions including planthouses in which can be found a large and varied collection of the world's flora, a Sussex Heritage Trail with handcrafted models of famous Sussex historical landmarks including castles, forts, mills and railways, a collection of huge replica dinosaurs in the Dinosaur Safari park, and some superb water gardens. Of particular interest, however, is the Museum of Life which provides the extraordinary life story of Planet Earth from its earliest beginnings. It is home to a unique collection of fossils, minerals and crystals which represent a lifetime of collecting from all the corners of the globe. Among the most prized exhibits are a fossil dinosaur egg laid 97 million years ago and a splendid fossil dinosaur footprint. The museum invites you to "unlock the secrets of the Earth's interior." There is a gift centre, café and lots of activities for children.

Tangmere Aviation Museum, *Tangmere, Chichester, West Sussex, tel 01243 775223*
Founded by a group of dedicated volunteers, this museum tells the story of this Battle of Britain airfield from its origins in 1916. It traces the development of the airfield through the air wars over southern England during World War 2 to the post-war period of the RAF High Speed Flight and the jet fighter squadrons that established their bases here. There is a unique collection of aviation exhibits and memories; of special interest are the world air speed record-breaking aircraft, namely Hunter, Swift and Meteor. The

visitor will also be able to experience the story of the first Spitfire prototype and its designer R.J. Mitchell, while children will enjoy the thrill of "flying" the aircraft simulators. The museum also contains a tranquil Memorial Garden and there is both a cafeteria and souvenir shop.

***Weald & Downland Open Air Museum, *Singleton, West Sussex, tel 01243 811348*
This remarkable museum in the heart of the Sussex countryside is effectively a collection of a large number of rural buildings, each with its own distinctive character and design, that have literally been reassembled in a delightful pastoral landscape, populated by hens, sheep and shire horses. By exploring the buildings, the visitor can find out how people lived and worked, and watch demonstrators at work using traditional skills such as milling and weaving. In the Downland Gridshell, the first timber gridshell building in the UK, can be found the Museum's conservation workshop and a fascinating collection of rural artefacts; the Winkhurst Kitchen complete with costumed cook, offers traditional Tudor food; and seven gardens show the greenery that met the everyday needs of rural households down the centuries. There are numerous special exhibitions and events during the year including the famous Food Fair in spring. Refreshments available.

TOP TEN TRADITIONAL RECIPES IN SUSSEX

Acres Pudding: So called because Sussex folk could reputedly eat it by the acre, its ingredients are 6 oz suet, 6 oz raisins, 6 oz flour and a quarter of a pint of milk. Simply mix the ingredients up well and bake it in a tin for one hour.

Chiddingly Hot Pot: You need 1 lb of beef, 8 oz celery, 8 oz olives, tarragon vinegar, mixed spices, 1 lb onions or shallots, 1 lb potatoes, cloves and black peppercorns. Chop the onions, celery and olives. Place a layer of onions on the bottom of a large casserole dish, together with some of the celery and olives. On top of them, place thin slices of beef and sprinkle with a little spice and vinegar. Cut the potatoes into thin slices and put the slices over the meat with more olives and celery; repeat till all the ingredients are used up. Pour enough water into the casserole so that the mixture is nearly covered, then cook in a low oven for between 3 and 4 hours, depending on the quantities used.

Herb Pie: You need 2 handfuls of parsley, 1 handful of spinach, 2 lettuces, mustard and cress, a few leaves of burridge, 2 eggs, flour, a pint of cream, half a pint of milk and some white beet leaves. Wash the herbs then boil them a little. Empty the water, press out the water from the herbs and cut the herbs into small pieces. Mix them up and place them in a dish sprinkled with salt. Mix a batter with flour, two eggs that are well beaten, the cream and the milk and pour the batter on to the herbs. Cover with a good crust and then bake.

Old Sussex Potato and Cheese Cakes: The ingredients are half a pound of cooked potatoes, 2 oz flour, 2 oz grated cheese, 1 egg, butter and salt. Mash the cooked potatoes with the salt and butter. To that, add the grated cheese, flour and the egg, well beaten. Mix it all together well, then roll out and make into small round cakes. Bake in the oven for about 12 minutes.

Sussex Bacon Pudding: There are two ways of making this dish. For the first method you need suet dough, sage and seasoning, chopped bacon, onion, swede and turnips; roll out the dough thinly and spread with the bacon, onion, sage and seasoning, roll it over and over as you would for a jam roly-poly, tie in a cloth and boil surrounded by the other vegetables. For the second method you need suet dough, chopped bacon (from 3 or 4 rashers), a chopped onion, chopped parsley, a little pepper and salt, teaspoon of mixed herbs, a little milk and a well-beaten egg: line a greased basin with the suet dough, mix up the other ingredients and place the mixture in the basin, covering with a lid of dough. Boil for 2 hours and serve with a thick gravy.

Sussex Currant & Apple Dumplings: Simply mix together the following ingredients: half a pound of flour, half a pound of suet, 2 oz sugar, 2 oz currants, a ripe apple that has been peeled, cored and diced, and a pinch of salt. Add a little sour milk or a little water, roll the mixture into dumplings, boil for 15 minutes, and dust with moist sugar. Serve with treacle.

Sussex Dripped Pudding: This is a pudding to accompany a Sunday roast, but unlike Yorkshire pudding this is made of suet. You need 6 oz suet, 1 lb plain flour, a teaspoon of baking powder and a pinch of salt. Shred the suet and mix with the flour, baking powder and salt, adding about half a pint of cold water. Tie into a flavoured cloth and boil for an hour. Remove from the cloth and cut into slices, then lay the slices in the dripping pan under the roasting meat, thereby allowing them to become saturated with the dripping and brown on top.

Sussex Mock Pork Pie: The ingredients are short or rough puff pastry, 2-3 oz bacon per person, 1 egg per person, half a teaspoon of mixed herbs, pepper and salt. Line a shallow pie dish with the pastry, then arrange the bacon pieces in it and dust with a pinch or more of thin herbs. Break the eggs, taking care to keep the yolks intact, and pour into the pie. Add seasoning, cover with more pastry and bake for an hour. Serve hot or cold.

***Sussex Plum Heavies: Described by Tony Wales as perhaps the most famous of all Sussex recipes, the ingredients for it are 2 oz lard, 2 cups of flour, 1 oz caster sugar, 2 oz currants or sultanas, and a cup of milk soured by adding the juice of half a lemon. Rub the lard into the flour. Add the sugar and fruit, followed by the soured milk, in order to create pastry from the mixture. Roll out and cut into small rounds. Brush over with the remainder of the milk. Bake for 15 mins in a moderate oven.

Sussex Pond Pudding: The ingredients are 8 oz suet dough, 4 oz Demerara sugar, a handful of currants, 4 oz butter, and a pinch of spice. Roll out the dough into a thick round shape about the size of a dinner plate. Then place in the centre a large ball of butter as well as the currants, spice and sugar. Pull the suet crust up round the butter ball to give the pudding the appearance of a large apple dumpling. Seal the top with a piece of suet crust, tie in a floured cloth and boil for between 2 and 2.5 hours. There are variations on this recipe, one of which involves placing a washed lemon, that has been pricked all over, into the middle of the ball of butter.

TOP TEN HISTORIC TOWNS IN SUSSEX

Arundel, West Sussex: The chief glory and dominant feature of Arundel is indisputably its castle. Most of it is in fact comparatively recent in origin, having been rebuilt in the eighteenth century on the site of a great medieval fortress; it has been the seat of the Dukes of Norfolk and the Earls of Arundel for more than 700 years. All that remains of the original fortification are the 12th century shell keep and fragments of the 13th century barbican and curtain wall. Close to the castle is the town's Roman Catholic cathedral, commissioned by the Fifteenth Duke of Norfolk and built in Gothic style in the 1870's, although it was only designated a cathedral in 1965. More or less opposite the cathedral is the much older parish church of St Nicholas, dating back to the 14th century, and divided by a screen into separate Anglican and Catholic areas. The Catholic chapel within the church is known as the Fitzalan Chapel where former Dukes of Norfolk and Earls of Arundel lie buried, and there are some most impressive canopied tombs. It was badly damaged in the English Civil War but has been magnificently restored. The town, built on a hill above the river Arun, contains many fine old buildings, particularly along Tarrant Street and Maltravers Street.

Battle, East Sussex: The site of the famous conflict in 1066 between King Harold and William Duke of Normandy, Battle's most important historical feature is its Abbey, owned by English Heritage. It was built by the victorious William in atonement for the blood he shed on the battlefield; the accommodation provided for those who constructed it constituted the town's beginnings. Although the Abbey itself is now a ruin, the Abbey gatehouse contains examples of Norman, Gothic and early Renaissance architecture. Abbey Green, in front of the gatehouse, is arguably the most picturesque part of the town, and includes the magnificent half-timbered Pilgrim's Rest, dating from the 15th century and latterly a restaurant. Other gems in Battle include the Friar House which dates back to 1642; the timber-framed Almonry, a hall-house with 15th century origins; the tile-hung Kings Head inn; and Langton House,

This food room in Battle, despite the date on it, used to be a Victorian chapel, dating back to the 1880's.

which was originally built in the 16th century as a two-storeyed half-timbered building, with another storey being added in around 1700 and a new front being put on later in the 18th century. The town has a magnificent museum, Yesterday's World, housed in a medieval hall-house.

***Chichester, West Sussex:** Chichester strictly does not belong in this category as technically it is a city, not a town. However it would be a travesty to omit it, as it is crammed with magnificent buildings, of which the greatest is its cathedral. It dates back to the end of the 11th century and is particularly noteworthy for its Norman sculptures, Arundel Screen, and shrine of St Richard. The focal point of Chichester is its market cross, built in 1501 by Bishop Story, and the meeting place of the four main streets: North Street with its 18th century Council House and the early 19th century Buttermarket, South Street with its Vicar's Hall which contains a late 12th century vaulted undercroft, East Street with its 16th century Royal Arms and early 19th century Corn Exchange, and West Street with its splendid 17th century redbrick Edes House. However, the side streets within Chichester's ancient walls, parts of which date back to AD100, contain many other gems, including the early 18th century Pallant House which is now an art gallery, the old St Mary's Hospital and chapel which saw occupancy by the Franciscans as long ago as the 13th century, the Vicars Close near the cathedral with 15th century houses, and the early 13th century Bishop's Palace. There is an excellent museum in Little London.

Hastings, East Sussex: Founded by the Saxons, Hastings was one of the original Cinque Ports and was already an important harbour town at the time of the Norman invasion. The old town grew up in a valley between two sandstone ridges, East Hill and West Hill, and on West Hill today can still be seen the ruins of a Norman castle. From West Hill narrow lanes lead steeply down to the centre of the old town, which is full of splendid buildings. Of seven medieval churches, two still remain, namely the early 15th century All Saints Church and St Clement's Church which was rebuilt following destruction by French invaders in 1390. Secular buildings of interest include East Hill House, Torfield and Old Hastings House, all of which date back to the 18th century, but there are many delightfully quaint houses in the picturesquely-named Tackleway, Rock-a-Nore Road, Winding Street and St Clement's Passage. The importance of Hastings' thriving fishing industry is reflected in the Fishermen's Museum and displays in the Old Town Hall Museum, while the St Clement's Caves recall the dangers that faced the Hastings smugglers. Hastings developed significantly as a seaside resort in the early 19th century, and west of the old town there are several fine Regency-style houses.

Lewes, East Sussex: The county town of East Sussex, Lewes is built on a steep chalk promontory at a crossing of the river Ouse. Its most ancient surviving building is the remnant of the Norman castle built by William the Conqueror's lieutenant

William de Warenne. The town was the scene of an important battle in 1264 between the forces of Henry III and Simon de Montfort. Later the town found itself the centre of what had become a substantial agricultural district and acquired considerable prosperity. Many fine buildings were erected early in the 19th century, and the main street is still lined today with splendid old timber-framed and brick-built town houses. Among the best are the Law Courts, the Museum of Sussex Archaeology adjoining the castle, and the superb timber-framed Fifteenth Century Bookshop. The area of Lewes known as Southover is also very rich in

With so many High Streets dominated by chain stores, the main street of Lewes boasts a distinctive character and beautiful hillside setting.

old town houses, including Anne of Cleves House, a timber-framed house dating back to 1500. Lewes has many old churches, of which the oldest is St Anne's, a solid Norman creation with a tower that dates back to 1150. William Cobbett described the town as a "model of solidity and neatness."

Midhurst, West Sussex: This little town lies on a sandstone ridge north of the Downs, 12 miles above Chichester. The town's main street is North Street, a bustling wide thoroughfare with many attractive shops and houses, several of which have Georgian facades. However the loveliest part of Midhurst is round the market square and church, linked to North Street via Knockhundred Row. The original town centre was situated round the market square and today it is a haven of peace, with beautiful old timber-framed and brick-built town houses, shops and inns. One of the finest buildings in this part of Midhurst is the Spread Eagle, a huge coaching inn with a sign claiming the date of 1430 although most of it is 17th century. The town library, in Knockhundred Row, is housed in another fine 17th century building. A short walk from the town centre, beside the picturesque river Rother, are the ruins of Cowdray House, at one time the most magnificent Tudor house in the whole of Sussex. The house was destroyed by fire in 1793 but the shell of the building survives and is a most impressive sight.

Petworth, West Sussex: Petworth might be described as the definitive Sussex country town, with narrow bustling streets, large imposing church, central square and a tremendous variety of town houses, the whole being watched over by a magnificent stately home. Petworth House is the undoubted jewel of the town, dating back more than 6 centuries although extensive rebuilding took place in the late 17th century to give it an almost chateau-like appearance. It is famed today for its magnificent paintings and is set in 700 acres of beautiful parkland. The church of St Mary has 13th century features, a curiously un-English red-brick tower, and some fine monuments including a life-size figure of George, Earl of Egremont. Of the many beautiful old town houses in Petworth, among the best are the 16th century Pettifers in the very picturesque Lombard Street; a huge Georgian mansion known as Daintrey House; the mid-17th century Stringers Hall with its fine bay windows; the late 15th century Sadlers Rest; the late 18th century Leconfield Hall on the square; George House, dating back to 1805; and the town museum, a 17th century building providing a fascinating insight into early 20th century cottage life.

Petworth's main square, dominated by Leconfield Hall, built in 1794 and formerly a court house.

Rye, East Sussex: This hilltop town, formerly a hill fort, became one of the Cinque Ports in the mid-14th century and was once a port of considerable strategic importance. The streets of the town, many of them cobbled and narrow, are crammed with historic houses, many weather-boarded, timber framed or tile-hung, and splendidly preserved. The town's focal point is St Mary's Church, which has a remarkable clock that it said to have the oldest functioning pendulum in England. Other particularly important features in Rye include the 14th century Landgate, the

The little town of Rye, with its beautiful hilltop setting, is a mecca for visitors all the year round.

last remaining of Rye's original fortified gates; the Ypres Tower, dating back to the 13th century and once a prison; the Mermaid Inn in the gorgeous cobbled Mermaid Street, with 13th century features; the 17th century Old Grammar School in the High Street, with distinctive Dutch gables; the 15th century timber-framed Flushing Inn; the 18th century arcaded Town Hall; the three-storey 15th century timber-framed Fletcher's House; the magnificent Lamb House, an 18th century building in West Street and home to the novelists Henry James and later E.F. Benson; and the fine Georgian brick-built Old Vicarage Hotel in East Street.

Steyning, West Sussex: Lying on the west bank of the river Adur, Steyning was once an important port and although Shoreham was later to become the main harbour of the Adur, the prosperity of Steyning was already assured. The port of Steyning was known as St Cuthman's after the saint who, on the death of his father, travelled across country bearing his crippled mother in a cart. The cart broke down on reaching Steyning and St Cuthman settled here. The town has an exceptionally interesting church, the parish church of St Andrew, boasting a late Norman nave with huge round columns and carved arches. Steyning has many very fine secular buildings also, most notably the Brotherhood Hall in Church Street, the original building of the Steyning Grammar School that was founded in 1614, and the Old Market House in the High Street. There are in the town a number of examples of 14th and 15th century hall houses, with the Post Office in the High Street being one of the best. Many of the

Church Street, Steyning. The tall brick building on the left is the Grammar School, founded in 1614.

buildings of Steyning use a laminated sandstone called Horsham stone for roof covering, but there are plenty of other building styles evident in the town, including tile-hanging, timber-framing and weather-boarding.

Winchelsea, East Sussex: The old town of Winchelsea stood at shore level on a shingle spit on the seaward side of where the town is today, and before the end of the 12th century it had become one of the Cinque Ports. Following a storm in 1287 which washed most of the old town away, a new town was built on the nearby hilltop. The grid street pattern of the new town made it effectively England's first piece of town planning, and the grid pattern can still be seen today. There are many fine buildings in Winchelsea including the medieval vaults which probably served as cellars for imported barrels of wine; the church of St Thomas with Sussex marble effigies and canopied and pinnacled tombs dating back to the early 14th century; the Armoury in Castle Street, also of 14th century origin; and the Court Hall, thought to date back to the first days of the "new" town and now containing a museum. The original street layout remains, with well spaced-out houses, some painted white, some tile-hung, and many decorated with climbing roses and wisteria. Among the prettiest is the 18th century New Inn in German Street. The town boasts three medieval gates, including Strand Gate which is early 14th century in origin.

TOP TEN NAMED FOOTPATHS IN SUSSEX

The Downs Link: As the name of this path suggests, it provides a link between the North Downs Way at St Martha's Hill, just east of Guildford, and the South Downs Way at Bramber, but in fact goes on beyond Bramber to Shoreham. The 37 mile walk begins in the lovely wooded countryside on and around the North Downs, but for most of its course follows two old railway lines, the Guildford-Horsham and the Horsham-Shoreham lines, via Bramley, Cranleigh, Rudgwick, Slinfold, Christ's Hospital, Southwater, Partridge Green, Henfield and Steyning. The path is extremely well marked, and for the most part very easy to follow. ROUTE PACK AVAILABLE BY CONTACTING 01243 777610.

The Downs Link, providing a walk between the North and South Downs, uses the course of two old railways for much of its journey.

The High Weald Landscape Trail: This trail runs for 90 miles between Horsham and Rye via East Grinstead: those passing through Horsham station may have seen signposts for the trail on the station itself! As its name suggests, it crosses the High Weald, an area of rolling and often wooded countryside between the North Downs and South Downs escarpments and now designated an Area of Outstanding Natural Beauty. The area is extremely rich archaeologically, architecturally, geologically and historically. There is a link between the route and five recommended circular walks. A beautifully produced book describing the route has been written by Eila Lawton and Lorna Jenner, ISBN 0953601307.

The Monarch's Way: This is, in its entirety, second only to the South West Coast Path as the longest continuous footpath in England, running as it does for a total of 610 miles. The route is so called because it follows the escape route of Charles II following his defeat at the Battle of Worcester in 1651. From Worcester the route proceeds via Stratford upon Avon to the Cotswolds and on through the Mendips to the Dorset coast at Charmouth. The route then goes eastwards close to the South coast all the way to Shoreham Harbour where Charles II made his escape to France. It passes through some of the finest scenery in Western and Southern England, and connects with three other paths in the top ten, namely the Sussex Border Path, South Downs Way and Downs Link. Three guide books set out the route in full. The book describing the Sussex section is written by Trevor Antill, ISBN 1869922298.

The Saxon Shore Way: Most of the 163 miles of the Saxon Shore Way run through Kent, following much of its coastline, but the last part of this journey from Gravesend to Hastings runs through Sussex. The majority of the route is along the flat, but the gently rolling surrounding countryside is most attractive, and the coastline itself offers salt marshes, white cliffs and a number of historic towns. The path is well documented and the Ordnance Survey (Aurum Press) has published a very full guide to the route written by Bea Cowan (ISBN 185410392X).

The South Downs Way.

***The South Downs Way: This is without doubt the finest named footpath in Sussex and the only route in Sussex that so far has National Trail status. It runs for 100 miles between Eastbourne and Winchester, in Hampshire, but it is undoubtedly far more rewarding to walk it from west to east. The national trail follows the South Downs escarpment, with magnificent views both northwards to the Weald and southwards to the sea throughout its journey. Its many scenic highlights include Harting Hill, Bignor Hill, Rackham Hill, Chanctonbury Ring, the extraordinary Devil's Dyke, arguably its finest viewpoint, Ditchling Beacon, Firle Beacon, the beautiful Cuckmere Haven, the spectacular Seven Sisters and the immensely popular Beachy Head. The path is exceedingly well defined and waymarked throughout, route finding is very easy, and there are ample accommodation and refreshment opportunities on or close to the route. The Ordnance Survey (Aurum Press) has published Paul Millmore's definitive guide to the route (ISBN 1854104071), but there are many other guides that are very easily available, including SB Publications' own book, *South Downs Way* by David Harrison.

The Sussex Border Path: This path runs for 135 miles, between Emsworth on the border between Sussex and Hampshire and Rye on the border between Sussex and Kent. The path aims to follow, as closely as possible, the border between Sussex and its neighbouring counties of Hampshire, Surrey and Kent, but the path rarely if ever goes along the border itself and frequently makes incursions into its neighbouring counties. The main attraction of the path is the fact that it is so unspoilt and remote, and that progressing from the sea across the Downs to the Weald and back to the sea again, there is a tremendous variety of scenery and terrain; the amount of signposting is variable and this makes the walk extra challenging. Sigma Leisure have published a book by John Allen describing the route, ISBN 1850586772.

The 1066 Country Walk: This is a 31 mile walk which links the historic East Sussex settlements of Rye and Pevensey, and as one might expect passes through Battle en route. As well as putting the walker more closely in touch with a very important part of our history, the journey passes through a variety of attractive scenery close to the Sussex coast. There are connections with two other "top ten" paths, the Saxon Shore Way and the South Downs Way, and there is a link route to Hastings. Although it is one of the newer "name paths" in Sussex, the route is clearly set out on Ordnance Survey maps. A guide to the route has been written by Brian Smailes, ISBN 1903568005.

The Vanguard Way: This is a 66-mile walk linking East Croydon, arguably best known for its important railway station, with Newhaven. It was devised in 1980 by members of the Vanguards Rambling Club based in Croydon. It begins by crossing over the North Downs then goes across the Greensand Ridge on the border between Surrey and Kent before proceeding southwards through the Weald to Ashdown Forest. Beyond the forest it continues to the Cuckmere valley at Alfriston via the Low Weald, and follows the valley to just below Seaford Head

Vanguard Way signpost.

before heading west along the coast to reach Newhaven. The variety of scenery is remarkable, but a guide book is essential as it is not properly waymarked on the ground. Publication: The Wealdway and Vanguard Way by Kev Reynolds, Cicerone 1987, ISBN 0902363859.

The Wealdway: The Wealdway is an 82-mile walk that starts at Gravesend in Kent, on the banks of the Thames, and finishes at Beachy Head overlooking Eastbourne and the Sussex coast. It runs via the North Downs to the Medway, then over a series of ridges of the High Weald and forward to Ashdown Forest. Beyond the forest the

Wealdway enters the Low Weald and continues to reach the South Downs with its marvellously climactic finish at Beachy Head. With its distinctive WW motif, it is well signposted. In terms of scenery and terrain, there are obvious similarities between this and the Vanguard Way. Publication: See Vanguard Way above.

The Wey South Path: This path, 36 miles long, starts from Guildford in Surrey and ends near Amberley where it meets the South Downs Way. Wherever possible, it follows the line of the Wey & Arun Canal, the central part of the link between the Thames at Weybridge and the Channel coast at Littlehampton; where the canal cannot be followed the route follows a disused railway as well as roads and footpaths. The Wey South Path joins the canal at Shalford and having risen to a wooded area round Loxwood enters Sussex and follows the valley of the River Arun. For a number of miles the path runs parallel both with the old canal and the Arun, forsaking the Arun near Pallingham but returning to it near Stopham and continuing close to the Arun past Pulborough, Greatham, Bury and Amberley. The beauty of the path is in its range of unspoilt scenery, from Surrey woodlands to lush water meadows with the backcloth of the chalk downs. A guide book by Geoff Perks and Ken Bacon is available, ISBN 0953191109.

TOP TEN RIVERS IN SUSSEX

A tranquil section of the Adur, one of the grandest rivers in Sussex.

The Adur, *Shipley/Burgess Hill-Shoreham by Sea, West Sussex*

The Adur has two sources. The western arm rises near Shipley, a few miles south-west of Horsham, and flows through tranquil farmland, across the lovely grounds of Knepp Castle and past the attractive villages of West Grinstead and Partridge Green, although not all of the bank is accessible to walkers. The eastern arm rises near Burgess Hill but only becomes properly accessible to visitors west of Wineham, where it enters the very picturesque Shermanbury Estate and its beauty is enhanced by weirs and tributary streams. The two arms meet near Henfield and the whole of the rest of the river can be followed along the east or the west bank. The river follows through delightfully unspoilt countryside, soon crossing the course of the Shoreham-Christ's Hospital railway and then proceeding towards the sea, with the beautiful South Downs escarpment as a backcloth. A build-up of houses and traffic noise signifies the approach to the virtually-joined-up communities of Steyning, Bramber and Upper Beeding. Beyond these villages the river passes beneath the busy Bramber by-pass and then back into more tranquil surroundings, with good views across to the fine old church of Botolphs. The river continues past the undoubted eyesore which is the Upper Beeding cement works, and on past the quite magnificent 19th century Lancing College Chapel and underneath the A27. The river then passes the historic church at Old Shoreham to the left, and Shoreham Airport to the right, shortly arriving in the bustling port of Shoreham by Sea where it flows into Shoreham Harbour.

The Arun, *Horsham-Littlehampton, West Sussex:*

Arguably the best-loved river in West Sussex, the Arun has rather unassuming beginnings, rising close to Horsham but meandering somewhat aimlessly at first and actually drifting away from the sea, widening near Rudgwick and then heading more resolutely seawards. From Rudgwick the Arun proceeds through agreeable but unspectacular farmland, but just north of Newbridge, between Billinghurst and

Wisborough Green, it is met by the Wey & Arun Junction Canal and proceeds close to the course of the old canal for many miles. It passes the extensive grounds of Pallingham Manor and the spectacular wooded hillsides just north of Stopham, but it is only beyond the fine old Stopham Bridge that the Arun matures into a truly impressive waterway. It turns eastwards to pass Pulborough and through the Pulborough Brooks Nature Reserve, then goes underneath the fine Greatham Bridge and on past Amberley Castle to Bury, from which the riverbank can be followed virtually all the way to the sea. The river crosses the South Downs Way just before Houghton Bridge, then having passed between the villages of Houghton and Amberley skirts the parkland and woodland of Arundel Park, passing the pretty hamlet of South Stoke, the popular Black Rabbit pub and an important wildfowl reserve before arriving at Arundel. The Arun at Arundel is one of the most photographed views in Sussex and is a popular destination for leisure craft travelling upstream from Littlehampton. The river passes close to the town's magnificent Gothic-style castle then continues serenely through the meadows past Ford and under the A259. Beyond the A259 the pastoral surroundings are left behind as the river enters the busy town of Littlehampton, flowing past the newly-developed waterfront round Pier Road to reach the English Channel.

The Brede, *Battle-Rye, East Sussex*

The Brede rises in the vicinity of the historic town of Battle and flows eastwards, passing under Sedlescombe Bridge just south of Sedlescombe, one of the prettiest villages in East Sussex. It continues eastwards under the A28 at Brede Bridge, and proceeds across Brede Level with Udimore to the north and Icklesham to the south. Now widening, it snakes round the north edge of the tiny town of Winchelsea, passing under the A259 at Strand Bridge. It goes eastwards passing the north end of the straggling village of Winchelsea Beach, then turns north and heads for Rye, flowing immediately parallel to the A259 Winchelsea-Rye road and going forward to meet the East Sussex Rother at Rye. Disappointingly there is little of the river available to be followed: there is a brief piece of riverside walking just to the east of Brede Bridge and between just north of Icklesham and Winchelsea, and simply by walking along the A259 between Winchelsea and Rye one can follow its latter stages.

The Cuckmere, *Cowbeech-Cuckmere Haven, East Sussex*

The Cuckmere, or Cuckmere River as it is popularly known, rises close to Cowbeech a few miles north-east of Hailsham. From Cowbeech it meanders through unspoilt countryside to Hellingly, passing under the Cuckoo Trail, the course of the old Polegate to Eridge railway line, and proceeds past the north-west tip of the sprawling community of Hailsham. It continues in a south-westerly direction past Lower Horsebridge, becoming wider and more impressive as it reaches the magnificent Michelham Priory; dating back to medieval times, the late Tudor buildings are

River Cuckmere.

sumptuously furnished with paintings and tapestries. Beyond Michelham, the Cuckmere continues south-westwards past Upper Dicker and Arlington, best known for its important reservoir, then near Berwick passes beneath the A27. South of the A27 the river, having thus flowed through scenery that has been tranquil but unremarkable, now enters an area of exceptional beauty, with the South Downs rising to the right and left. It flows past the beautiful village of Alfriston and only from here is it possible to start walking beside the river bank. The Cuckmere passes the pretty village of Litlington and continues on to Exceat Bridge where it goes underneath the A259 coast road and on past the Golden Galleon pub into the very special area known as Cuckmere Haven. From here it is a short distance to the sea. This estuarine landscape is hugely popular with walkers and naturalists, and is the last truly unspoilt estuary in Sussex, with Seaford Head rising up to the right, the Seven Sisters to the left, and barely a building in sight.

The Ems, *Walderton-Emsworth, West Sussex*
The Ems is the shortest of the top ten rivers nominated, but a river of real beauty and contrasts. Like the River Lavant, its flow is dependent on substantial winter rainfall. Rising at Mitchmere, a short distance north of the pretty village of Walderton, it flows down to and through the middle of Walderton, then flows roughly parallel with the main Funtington-Petersfield road, past the impressive buildings of Lordington. Passing a road junction, where following heavy rain the accumulation of waters in the surrounding fields makes a particularly appealing sight, the river flows on past the village of Racton, with its part-12th century church and extraordinary redbrick folly known as Racton Tower. Beyond Racton the Ems continues through most attractive

rolling pastures, passing underneath the road and going forward to and underneath the Funtington-Rowlands Castle road. From here it runs more or less parallel with Foxbury Lane to arrive at the sprawling but pretty village of Westbourne, being joined by a tributary stream that is fed by ponds near the hamlet of Aldsworth. The river flows through the middle of Westbourne, dominated by its 14th century church, then strikes out into open fields which are rudely interrupted by the new A27 road. Beyond the A27 the river enters Brook Meadow, a wildlife sanctuary with a pleasing mix of meadows and woodland, then passes beneath the A259 and emerges close to its mouth on the edge of Chichester Harbour at the attractive town of Emsworth. There are no footpaths signposted along the river bank, apart from a brief section in Brook Meadow, but much of the river can be followed from nearby paths or roads.

The Lavant, *East Dean-Appledram, West Sussex*

This capricious river begins its journey to the sea at East Dean, not far from Singleton about 8 miles north of Chichester. It flows roughly parallel with the minor road linking East Dean and Singleton, running past the pretty village of Charlton and its popular Fox Goes Free pub. At Singleton, a most attractive village with a pond, fine flint cottages and one of the best museums in Sussex, the river begins following a parallel course with the A286, initially to the west of this road and then passing underneath it

into the magnificent gardens of West Dean College. The river flows along the bottom end of the village of West Dean, the parallel road providing a grandstand view of the waters, then strikes out towards the villages of Mid and East Lavant. For much of this part of the journey it is within sight of the old Chichester to Midhurst railway, this section of which has become a popular footpath and cycle way. The river flows behind the village of Mid Lavant and through the middle of East Lavant, parallel with Sheepwash Lane, then heads out into open countryside again between the broad expanse of Goodwood Airfield and the district of Summersdale on the edge of Chichester. The river then enters Chichester, passing along the south edge of the city and emerging by the College, then proceeds past the Terminus Road industrial estate, under the A27, and serenely on

The River Lavant in full flow in the picturesque surroundings of West Dean near Chichester.

to Chichester Harbour close to the village of Appledram. It is a winterbourne stream, normally flowing only during the winter months;

some years it does not flow at all but when it does flow the result can be dramatic. Twice in recent years it has flooded spectacularly, most notably in January 1994 when overflowing waters engulfed the East Lavant village green. The river is particularly noteworthy for its beautiful flint-built bridges.

***The Ouse, *Haywards Heath-Newhaven*

The Ouse rises close to Lindfield on the edge of Haywards Heath in West Sussex, and heads eastwards under East Mascalls Bridge, soon reaching and proceeding close to the Bluebell Railway. It passes under the A275 Lewes-East Grinstead road by means of Sheffield Bridge, close to the beautiful Sheffield Park Gardens, then continuing south-eastwards, flows under Fletching Mill Bridge just south of Fletching village. The river crosses beneath the A272 just east of Newick at Gold Bridge, heads east to Sharpsbridge, and then turns southwards. It passes a little to the west of Isfield close to its confluence with the Uck, going down to Barcombe Mills; the Anglers Rest pub at Barcombe Mills is one of the most picturesque riverside pubs in Sussex. Now the Ouse swings south-westwards, passes the pretty village of Hamsey and gets to within sight of the Lewes-London railway, then swings gracefully south-eastwards and proceeds round the edge of Lewes. Passing under the A27, it then glides past the delightful villages of Rodmell, Southease and Piddinghoe, widening as it arrives at Newhaven with its busy harbour. A little to the south of Newhaven town the Ouse flows into the Channel; close to the mouth of the river is Newhaven Fort, which houses an impressive museum. A footpath following the whole of the Ouse was due to open in May 2005, and a guide to the route has recently been published, making it the most accessible of all the Sussex rivers and the most rewarding to explore.

The Rother (East Sussex), *Cross-in-Hand-Camber, East Sussex*

The East Sussex Rother rises in the heart of Wealden countryside not far from the beautiful village of Mayfield, and initially flows eastwards immediately to the north of the ridge on which Burwash is built. Passing Witherenden Mill it continues close to the main London-Hastings railway and goes forward to Etchingham, passing beneath the A265 Heathfield-Hurst Green road. Continuing south-eastwards, it proceeds on to the attractive community of Robertsbridge, then strikes out eastwards past the lovely village of Salehurst, with its very prominent church, under the B2244, and on to Bodiam. Between Robertsbridge and Bodiam, the Rother is running very close to the old railway line that linked Robertsbridge and Tenterden, and indeed the preserved section of this line at Robertsbridge is known as the Rother Valley railway. Beyond Bodiam, with its impressive castle, the Rother flows up to the A28 at Newenden, and beyond Newenden continues to the north of Peasmarsh. Hitherto very little of the river has been accessible but it now becomes followable using the Sussex Border Path. Meeting the Royal Military Canal near the B2082 Wittersham Road, the Rother turns sharply south-westwards and, taking the Sussex Border Path and Saxon Shore Way with it, goes down to Rye. From Rye it flows south-eastwards past Rye Golf Club to the left and Rye Harbour village to the right, arriving at the sea near Camber. This latter section of the river, followable for its most part along banks and through the sands, is impressively wide and was formerly a vital route for ships bringing goods to Rye.

The Rother (West Sussex), *Durford Mill-Hardham, West Sussex*

The West Sussex Rother, the longest river in Sussex that does not flow into the sea, actually rises a few miles north of Petersfield in Hampshire, entering West Sussex just east of Petersfield close to Durford Mill and proceeding eastwards just south of the village of Rogate, going forward to the twin settlements of Dumpford and Trotton. Passing under the A272 at Trotton, the Rother enters quite delightful countryside just south of Chithurst and heads eastwards through the village of Iping and just north of Stedham. The meadows and woodlands east of Stedham provide some of the loveliest riverside scenery in Sussex. The river passes under the lovely Woolbeding Bridge and the village of Woolbeding, then continues eastwards to the bustling old town of Midhurst, going under the A286 Chichester-Haslemere road. Leaving the town via the extensive Cowdray Estate and the ruins of Cowdray Castle, it meanders through gentle meadow scenery under Ambersham Bridge, and on just south of Tillington and Petworth. Proceeding under the A285 Chichester-Petworth road and passing the late 18th century Coultershaw Beam Pump, the Rother goes on eastwards under Shopham Bridge and through the meadows past Coates and Fittleworth and roughly parallel with the old Pulborough-Midhurst road. At length it arrives at Hardham, just west of Pulborough, where it flows into the Arun. There is some excellent riverside walking available between Trotton and Woolbeding and between Shopham Bridge and Fittleworth, but it is very patchy elsewhere.

The Uck, *Huggett's Furnace-Isfield, East Sussex*

The Uck only hit the headlines in 2000 when it caused spectacular flooding to the town of Uckfield. It rises in tranquil but unspectacular countryside between Mayfield and Buxted, Huggett's Furnace just north-east of Buxted being a point where a number of tributary streams converge to form the Uck itself. The Uck flows in a westerly direction through attractive meadow scenery, passing Howbourne Farm and then swinging south-westwards, parallel with the Oxted-Uckfield railway. It passes under the A272 immediately to the west of Uckfield and enters the very attractive Buxted Park, going forward through the sprawling town of Uckfield and running past a busy suburban industrial estate. It goes under the A26 and once again the surroundings become unspoilt as it meanders through the meadows close to the disused Lewes-Uckfield railway. It passes the village of Isfield and flows into the Ouse a short distance to the west of this village. Very little bank-side walking is available, the best sections being close to its confluence with the Ouse and just east of Howbourne Farm, although it can be enjoyed from a distance in Buxted Park.

TOP TEN CASTLES IN SUSSEX

Amberley, *near Arundel, West Sussex*
This square-towered castle was built by Bishop Rede of Chichester in the 1370's to defend the upper reaches of the Arun valley. However, it soon acquired a domestic character, being a summer retreat for bishops, and in fact was destined never to see military action. Its moment of glory was on the 14th October 1651 when legend has it that Charles II stayed here in the course of his flight to France after the Battle of Worcester, under the protection of Sir John Briscoe. The castle is not open to the public, now being part of an exclusive hotel and restaurant, but can be seen from the B2139 road as it passes the nearby village of Amberley, and features as one of the Top Ten Places To Stay in Sussex.

Arundel, *West Sussex, tel 01903 883136*
This castle had medieval origins, but little of the medieval castle now remains. Essentially, the castle, which looks so impressive today and which dominates the attractive little town around it, is a 19th century Gothic creation commissioned by the 15th Duke of Norfolk. The castle and estate had in fact been passed to the family of the Dukes of Norfolk and has been their seat since the 19th century. It was besieged by the Parliamentary army during the English Civil War and fell into decay, and it was not until 1800 that it was fully restored, then rebuilt between 1890 and 1903. Features of the castle of particular interest to modern visitors include a splendid mahogany library which survived the restorations, and paintings by Gainsborough, Reynolds, Van Dyck and Holbein. The castle is open to the public at certain times but, at the time of writing, not on Saturdays.

Bodiam, *near Robertsbridge, East Sussex, tel 01580 830436*
Following the sacking of Rye by the French in 1377, there was a real fear that the French might try and sail a flotilla further inland by means of the river Rother. Accordingly, an application was made by Sir Edward Dalyngrydge to build a castle here to guard against further French adventurism. Although permission was granted by the King, and the castle was duly built in 1385, the threatened French attack never materialised; it was not until the English Civil War that serious damage was done to the castle by hostile forces, but thereafter the castle fell into decay. It was rescued by Mad Jack Fuller of Brightling (see Top Ten Bizarre Landmarks in Sussex), serious restoration work followed at the end of the 19th century, and subsequently the property was acquired by the National Trust. Today a number of impressive features can still be seen by visitors including the gatehouse with portcullis, great hall, servants' hall, chapel and kitchen. There is also an excellent museum, and the grounds are particularly lovely. It is described as a "story book castle, the best example of its type in the country."

Bramber, *near Steyning, West Sussex*
Bramber Castle was built by William de Braose, a trusted lieutenant of William the

The noble ruin of Bramber Castle. Built by the Normans, it was destroyed in the Civil War.

Conqueror, soon after the Norman invasion. He chose what was a massive natural chalk outcrop towering over the valley of the river Adur; the water from the river would come right up to the castle walls and in fact the Norman soldiers built quays for goods and passengers. During the Middle Ages the castle saw many important visitors including King John in 1216, and Edward I between 1285 and 1302. The castle was all but destroyed by the Parliamentary army during the English Civil War and only a fragment of it now survives. It is very easily accessible although the best view of it is from a distance.

Camber, Rye, *East Sussex*

This was a fortress ordered by Henry VIII to be built to defend England against the French. Built in 1539 round an earlier tower, the castle had a stone exterior with brick-faced inner walls and a central tower with Tudor roses carved on the walls, and there was a platform for the mounting and firing of cannons. At its peak of activity in 1542 it had a garrison of forty-two. In 1642 the main fortifications were demolished and with the silting of the nearby river the castle became what Simon Jenkins calls a "romantic ruin." Today its ruins can only be reached on foot, set as it is among the dunes about a mile south of Rye (and nowhere near the present village of Camber).

Hastings, *East Sussex, tel 01424 718776*

Hastings Castle was the first stone structure built by the Normans after their invasion. All that remains today is part of the curtain wall, the lower sections of the western gatehouse, a few arches and part of the tower of the collegiate church. The original motte also survives in the angle of the curtain wall, but no keep remains, and one assumes that it collapsed when the cliffs on which the castle was built eroded. Outside the curtain wall visitors can still see passages in the sandstone, and although the reality is that these were probably storehouses, it is perhaps more exciting and romantic to think of them as dungeons. The castle ruin is today one of the town's most popular visitor attractions.

Herstmonceux, *near Hailsham, East Sussex, tel 01323 883816*

Originally built in 1440, Herstmonceux was one of the first and one of the largest brick buildings in England. For many years it was the home of the Fiennes family and during the 19th century it was the home of the writer Augustus Hare, it being passed to him by somewhat eccentric ancestors. One of these concocted a legend of a 9ft tall ghostly drummer to ward off inquisitive visitors! In the 1770's the interior was largely dismantled to build Herstmonceux Place but during the 1930's it was splendidly restored by the Lewes architect W.H. Godfrey; fortunately the original battlements and turrets remain to this day. It is set among carefully maintained Elizabethan gardens and parkland, and is still protected by a moat which gives the whole scene the appearance of a very traditional English castle. Though the grounds are open to the public, the castle is not, although guided tours are conducted at certain times.

Knepp, *near Horsham, West Sussex*

Like Bramber, Knepp Castle was built by William de Braose and was in fact a subsidiary castle to his main headquarters at Bramber. Used as a hunting lodge, it was the favourite residence of King John, but after his death in 1216 it ceased to be fortified. It remained as a residence until the end of the 13th century then gradually became a ruin, and during the 18th century nearly all the remaining stone was removed and used to build a road. Today, all that is left is a portion of wall on a grassy mound surrounded by a moat; to quote John Godfrey, "with its weathercock and sprouting buddleia the remaining fragment of Knepp Castle is one of the most evocative ruins in the county." Most modern-day travellers, speeding along the immediately adjacent A24, will miss this most unusual feature altogether. A public footpath brings visitors to within sight of it at no cost.

Lewes, *East Sussex, tel 01273 486290*

With the mouth of the Ouse so close by, this was an obvious place for a Norman stronghold and indeed Lewes Castle was built by another trusted lieutenant of William the Conqueror, William de Warenne. It was a most unusual structure in that it was built on two mottes or artificial mounds, and a magnificent barbican or outer gatehouse was added early in the 14th century. Notwithstanding the Battle of Lewes between Henry III and Simon de Montfort in 1264, the castle was never besieged but instead succumbed to natural causes. Most of it was pulled down in 1620 and the stone

Lewes Castle dates back to about 1100; its barbican is described as "one of the mightiest....in England."

from the castle was sold at 4d per load, then in the 18th century the keep was turned into a summerhouse. Today the castle is owned by the Sussex Archaeological Society and is open to visitors, who even though they cannot appreciate the castle as it was in its heyday can still see some of de Warenne's original work and of course enjoy the superb hilltop setting.

***Pevensey, *near Eastbourne, East Sussex, tel 01323 762604*

The original Pevensey Castle was the Roman fortress Anderida which was built about 280 AD, and after the Romans left, the fortress was occupied in turn by the British, the South Saxons and King Alfred. Amazingly, much of the Roman walling still survives today. Following the Battle of Hastings a formidable Norman castle was erected inside the Roman walls by the Count of Mortain to whom William the Conqueror had entrusted the Rape of Pevensey; the keep was built around 1100 and the gatehouse was added in the 13th century. Withstanding sieges in 1088 and again in 1264, it continued to be garrisoned until the 14th century but was subsequently refortified during the time of the Spanish Armada and again during the Second World War. Much of the inner bailey survives including the base of the gatehouse, and the battlements, towers and dungeons of the medieval castle ruins can still be inspected today. It is now without doubt Pevensey's most celebrated visitor attraction.

TOP TEN VILLAGES IN SUSSEX

Alfriston, *near Seaford, East Sussex*
Formerly a market town, Alfriston stands on the site of a Saxon settlement adjacent to the Cuckmere River. Its narrow High Street boasts many medieval buildings, and the 14th century church, in a beautiful setting between a large green and the Cuckmere, has been described as the Cathedral of the South Downs; its stonework of small, square, knapped flints is most unusual in Sussex churches. Among the fine old secular buildings of the village, built in an assortment of styles and materials over the centuries such as tile-hanging, weatherboarding, brick and timber, there are some particularly interesting inns. The Market Cross Inn was the base of the infamous Alfriston Gang of smugglers, while the Star boasts ceiling timbers that are decorated with carved animals. On a street corner beside the Star stands a large red lion, which is the former figurehead of a 17th century Dutch ship, and on the edge of the green stands the 14th century Clergy House, acquired by the National Trust in 1896 and the first building the Trust bought.

Alfriston Village.

Amberley, *near Arundel, West Sussex*
Described as having a "lovely hodge-podge of styles," this village, with a beautiful setting close to the South Downs and the waters of the river Arun, boasts a massive variety of houses of all ages and styles, including flint, timber and tile along its winding

streets, which it has been said "coax…the visitor round each bend just to see what will happen next." Much of St Michael's Church dates from just after the Norman Conquest, and was the work of Bishop Luffa who founded Chichester Cathedral; among its most notable features are the twelfth century wall paintings of Christ In Majesty and the Resurrection.

Bignor, *near Pulborough, West Sussex*

The little village of Bignor consists of farms and cottages spaced round a rough square of four lanes at the foot of the South Downs. It does not have the "chocolate box" feel of some other Sussex villages, its interest lying in the beautiful Downland setting and variety of features. Facing on to one lane is the much-photographed 15th century

thatched house known as the Yeoman's House, with its frame of old timbers and in-filling of brick, flint and plaster; there is a pretty part-Norman and part-13th century church, guarded by an ornate lychgate and two massive yews; and there are a number of impressive houses around the four lanes including Ivy Cottage, Corner Cottage and another with a lovely stream flowing through its back garden. The feature which draws many visitors to Bignor is the Roman villa which was discovered in 1811 and is especially noteworthy for its mosaic work. The 82ft mosaic pavement is in fact the longest of its type in the British Isles, and the mosaic floors depict the Seasons and the heads of legendary figures such as the Medusa and the Ganymede. A short but very steep drive southwards up on to Bignor Hill brings you to the South Downs Way and

The lovely village of Bosham, near Chichester, boasts the beautiful Holy Trinity Church. King Harold received communion here in 1064.

also on to Stane Street, one of the most important thoroughfares of Roman times in this part of the country.

Bosham, *near Chichester, West Sussex*

One of the loveliest coastal settlements in the south of England, Bosham has roots in Roman times; not only are there Roman features in Holy Trinity Church but it is now known that a Roman villa was built here in Antoninus' reign. The church itself is one of the oldest sites of Christian worship in the whole of Sussex, with parts of it dating back to before the Norman Conquest. It boasts a Saxon tower and chancel, there are bases of a Roman arch in situ beneath the chancel arch, and there is an early 12th century crypt as well as a magnificent Early English east window of the same period. Its most famous communicant was King Harold who worshipped here before setting off to meet the future William the Conqueror in 1064, and Harold's arrival in Bosham is commemorated in the Bayeux Tapestry. Legend has it that King Canute lived for a time in Bosham and may even have tried to demonstrate his mastery of the waves from

here! Although there are few surviving ancient buildings in the village, there are some houses that date back to the 17th and 18th centuries with many attractive red brick, stone and flint buildings. The village used to have a thriving oyster trade and shipbuilding industry, but its chief industries now are tourism and sailing. Its setting, on the shores of a tidal creek of Chichester Harbour, is magnificent, and enhanced still further when the tide is in and the waters lap the beautiful green of Quay Meadow.

***Burwash,

near Heathfield, East Sussex
Described by more than one commentator as an outstandingly attractive village, the main street at Burwash, built

Burwash, once the home of Rudyard Kipling, boasts many lovely buildings including this fine church, the tower of which is Norman.

on a Wealden ridge, boasts an almost unbroken line of fine old shops and houses. Three centuries ago it was an important century of the iron industry and in St Bartholomew's Church at the eastern end of the village is a 14th century iron tomb slab claimed to be one of the oldest of its kind in the country; the church also has a Norman west tower and a very wide Early English chancel. Among the best of the 17th and 18th century timber framed and weatherboarded houses is the handsome timber-framed Rampyndene which dates back to 1699. A short distance from the village centre is Bateman's, a stone mansion originally built in 1634 and bought by Rudyard Kipling who lived there until his death in 1936. The house is open to visitors and contains many memorabilia of Kipling's life including his 1928 Rolls which sits proudly in the garage.

Ditchling, *near Lewes, East Sussex*
With its lovely setting between the South Downs escarpment and Ditchling Beacon a short way south, and the 188 acre nature reserve/country park to the north, Ditchling is full of interest for the browser and the historian. The lands around Ditchling were once part of a royal estate belonging to King Alfred who is believed to have owned a small palace here. The palace has now gone, but among features of interest to the contemporary visitor are the church of St Margaret of Antioch with its shingled Sussex cap spire, rare chalk carvings and Norman treasure chest; an unusual Tudor house called Wing's Place built of flint, timber and brick; the Regency house Cotterlings; Court Farm, which incorporates a village green and foundations of an old tithe barn; and the Old Meeting House, a centre of non-conformist worship dating from times when non-conformists could not worship within 5 miles of a town. The former village school contains an excellent museum with displays on Sussex history, rural life, period costumes and domestic interiors, and the Turner Dumbrell Workshops, in which traditional country crafts are carried on, are also well worth visiting.

Lindfield, *near Haywards Heath, West Sussex*
Despite having effectively become a suburb of Haywards Heath, this village has retained both an identity of its own and a remarkable number of really fine old buildings, many of them medieval in origin. The street, which drops down to a pond and large common, boasts buildings with timber framing, tile-hanging and elegant 18th century brickwork. Among the many highlights of this village, which owed its prosperity to traditional industries including paper, gloves and candles, are an old coaching inn, the Tiger, which although no longer an inn retains its original name to this day and has a fine red brick façade and timber-framed sides; the Old Place, another superb timber-framed house with its massive roof of local Horsham slate; the 18th century brickbuilt Lindfield Place; and the 14th century parish church with shingled spire.

The charming village of Lindfield retains its identity despite being so close to the busy commuter town of Haywards Heath.

Mayfield, *near Heathfield, East Sussex*

This Wealden village, now mercifully bypassed by the very busy A267, enjoys an exceptional variety of brick, stone and timbered houses. Amongst its most noteworthy buildings is the 15th century sandstone gatehouse which guards the remains of what used to be a palace of the Archbishops of Canterbury. Around the gatehouse and the palace remains has been built a convent school, but the medieval hall, its roof supported by huge stone arches, remains intact. Virtually opposite the gatehouse is Yeomans, a partially-altered example of a 15th century Wealden hall-house. The church, parts of which date back to the 13th century, contains some fine stone carvings, a 17th century font, some 17th/18th century monuments to the Baker family, and a Jacobean pulpit. The church is dedicated to St Dunstan, the Saxon Archbishop of Canterbury and founder of the original palace; legend has it that Dunstan had a number of confrontations with the Devil, and on one occasion disposed of him using a pair of red-hot tongs. Of the many splendid buildings that line the High Street, regarded as one of the finest in East Sussex, arguably the best is Middle House, converted from an oak-beamed Tudor residence to a popular country inn.

Rottingdean, *near Brighton, East Sussex*

Though on the coast, Rottingdean was historically more important as an agricultural settlement than as a fishing community. Now it is a very popular place for Brighton residents to come and unwind, with its timeless atmosphere, charming valley setting, easy access to the seafront, fine old buildings and good shops and restaurants. There are a number of excellent old flint, brick and timbered houses, as well as a charming green and pond. The flint Church of St Margaret is of Saxon foundation, and some pre-Conquest work survives in the nave. The earliest complete non-religious building in Rottingdean is the Black Horse, believed to date back to 1513, and a popular meeting place for smugglers. A number of very distinguished people have stayed or lived in Rottingdean, including Rudyard Kipling, the Irish Unionist leader Edward Carson and also Edward Burne-Jones who was responsible for the glorious colouring and design of the windows in the chancel of the church. Just outside the village is the Jacobean-style Roedean, the most famous of all girls' independent schools, and an 18th century smock mill which was once used to store contraband goods and which, with its four sails, has formed an important landmark to fishermen at sea.

West Hoathly, *near East Grinstead, West Sussex*
Set in wooded country just to the west of Ashdown Forest, and with panoramic views towards the South Downs, West Hoathly manages, in the words of one commentator, to "pack a remarkable number of historic buildings into a small space." Among its features of interest are the part-Norman St Margaret's Church which boasts a 12th century font, an early 15th century tower, a gigantic chest thought to date back to the 12th century, and 6-terraced churchyard; the 15th century timber-framed Priest House with a roof of huge Horsham stone slabs, now a folk museum containing country furniture, kitchen equipment, needlework and household items, and boasting a delightful garden; a 17th century manor house; and the 16th century Cat Inn, said to be a favourite spot for smugglers, and round which a number of old tile-hung cottages are clustered including the splendid 15th century hall-house Combers.

TOP TEN LITERARY PILGRIMAGES IN SUSSEX

Burwash, *near Heathfield, East Sussex*
Just below the ridge on which the village is built can be found Bateman's, a fine 17th century stone house in which Rudyard Kipling lived from 1902 until his death in 1936. He wrote some of his greatest work here including *Puck Of Pook's Hill* and the Sussex poems. The house, which is owned by the National Trust, is open to the public; arguably the most interesting room is the study, which today looks very much as he left it, with raised chair, long table with pipe-cleaners and inkwell, and books lining the walls.

Bury, *near Pulborough, West Sussex*
Bury House in the village was the home of John Galsworthy, author of *The Forsyte Saga,* from 1926 until his death in 1933. Like Virginia Woolf, he bought his Sussex house as a retreat from the pressures of London life, and little if any of his work was inspired by the Sussex landscape.

Felpham, *near Bognor Regis, West Sussex*
The poet William Blake lived in Felpham between 1800 and 1803, having initially come here to do some engraving for one William Hayley who lived in the village. Blake, who called the village "the sweetest spot on earth," settled in a white-walled thatched cottage to be found, appropriately enough, in Blake's Road, and claimed that during his stay in the village he saw a fairy's funeral in his garden. It was during his stay in Felpham that he wrote the words of the hymn *Jerusalem.* In a separate poem, he wrote of the village "Away to sweet Felpham, for Heaven is there; the ladder of angels descends through the air."

Hartfield, *East Sussex*
The clue to the importance of Hartfield in the world of literature lies in Pooh Corner, a shop which specialises in Winnie The Pooh gifts and memorabilia. A.A. Milne, the author of the Pooh books, lived near the village at Cotchford Farm on the edge of Ashdown Forest. The forest itself was the setting for the Pooh stories, and a bridge over a stream near the village is believed to have been the inspiration for the game of Poohsticks. The Pooh Corner shop at Hartfield is in fact 300 years old and was a sweet shop to which A.A. Milne's son Christopher, the inspiration for Christopher Robin of the stories, was taken by his nanny.

Lewes, *East Sussex*
Thomas Paine, who wrote *Rights Of Man,* lived at the 15th century half-timbered Bull House in the town from 1768 to 1774, working as an exciseman and a tobacconist. In the evenings he would go to the White Hart in the centre of the town and engage in earnest debate on the key political issues of the day. The diarist John Evelyn was educated at the town's Grammar School and lived for a time at the Grange in

Southover, which is part of Lewes itself. A little way out of Lewes, in Ringmer, there is a village sign depicting a tortoise called Timothy, who belonged to the aunt of the famous naturalist Gilbert White. When the naturalist visited Ringmer he became so fascinated with Timothy's activities that he took the tortoise back to Selborne and wrote about him in his immortal book *The Natural History Of Selborne*. A couple of miles north of Ringmer is Barcombe Mills; it was at East Crink, on the edge of Barcombe Mills, that Anthony Buckeridge lived and wrote many of his Jennings books, considered to be among the best school stories ever written. Dunhambury, the town featuring in the books, was loosely based on Lewes, and the surrounding downland inspired many of the incidents featured in the stories.

Midhurst, *West Sussex*

The author H.G. Wells was a pupil and schoolmaster at Midhurst Grammar School and whilst teaching there he lodged over a sweet shop next to the Angel Hotel in North Street. (Incidentally, the shop is now a tearoom featuring in the Top Ten Tearooms In Sussex elsewhere in this book.) As a child, Wells was apprenticed to Samuel Cowap, a chemist in what is now Church Hill, and he drew on his time with Mr Cowap in writing his novel *Tono-Bungay* (the strange title is the name of a patent medicine) in which Midhurst was rechristened Wimblehurst. Wells loved Midhurst, and the town is the background of several of his short stories; in his 1924 work *The Dream* there are mentions of the chemist shop and the school. Three blue plaques have been erected in the town in his honour. Wells spent part of his childhood at Uppark, the big house on the Downs above South Harting about 8 miles south-west of Midhurst. His mother was a maid at the house, and both Uppark and South Harting formed the inspiration for some of his work, with South Harting being named Siddermorton. Incidentally, South Harting was the home of Anthony Trollope, best known for his *Barchester Chronicles*, and in the village church may be found his letter scales, paperknife and pen. Just west of Midhurst, a mile or so upstream on the Rother, is Woolbeding where the Restoration dramatist Thomas Otway spent his youth in his father's rectory. He was born a few miles to the west in the village of Trotton in 1652 and he is commemorated by a tablet on the south wall of the chancel in Trotton's church.

Rodmell, *near Lewes, East Sussex*

In this small village of flint cottages in the Ouse valley between Lewes and Newhaven, the novelist Virginia Woolf had a country retreat at Monk's House from 1919 to 1941. She lived here with her husband Leonard, whilst not residing in Bloomsbury, London. The couple paid just £700 for the house which when they purchased it had no water, gas or electricity. They furnished the house with paintings, books and furniture similar to that at nearby Charleston, a house near Firle a few miles to the east where her artist sister Vanessa Bell lived. Tragically

Monk's House, Rodmell.

Virginia Woolf committed suicide in 1941 by drowning herself in the Ouse, and her ashes were scattered in the garden of Monk's House.

***Rye, *East Sussex*

Rye has been the home of a large number of important literary figures. The New York born novelist Henry James lived at Lamb House in West Street from 1898 till his death in 1916 and wrote some of his finest novels there; E.F. Benson, author of the *Mapp & Lucia* books, took over Lamb House after James' death and used Rye as the setting for the *Mapp & Lucia* series, calling the town Tilling; the poet Patric Dickinson lived at 38 Church Square; the golf writer Bernard Darwin lived at the Dormy House, just beside the Landgate; the dramatist John Fletcher was born in Fletcher's House in 1579; the children's author and creator of the *Captain Pugwash* books, John Ryan, has been for many years a resident of Gungarden Lodge at the corner of Church Square; the Forecastle at the end of Hucksteps Row was the home of Marguerite Radclyffe Hall, the controversial lesbian novelist, between 1928 and 1940; and the American novelist and poet Conrad Aiken lived in Jeake's House in Mermaid Street during the Depression years. Both the novelist Rumer Godden and the biographer Montgomery Hyde also stayed some time at Lamb House.

Shipley, *near Horsham, West Sussex*
Shipley was the home of Hilaire Belloc between 1906 and his death in 1953. Hilaire Belloc is perhaps most famous for his Cautionary Verse for children but was also a prolific writer about Sussex. He lived in a house called King's Land on the edge of the village, and he actually had his own windmill at the end of his garden. The mill was restored after his death and is now one of the finest mills in the South of England. On strolling around the village with its beautiful church near the mill, it is easy to see how Belloc gained inspiration for so much of his work; it remains an amazingly tranquil and unspoilt village in the heart of the Sussex countryside. Note that less than ten minutes' drive from Shipley, just across the A24, is West Grinstead, and it is in West Grinstead Park that Alexander Pope is reputed to have written much of *The Rape Of The Lock,* while a few miles up the A24 just beyond Horsham is Warnham, with which the poet Percy Shelley is associated. He was born at Field Place just outside the village, and a copy of the entry of his baptism in the village church has been displayed in its south aisle.

Worthing, *West Sussex*
A plaque on the Esplanade marks the site of the house where Oscar Wilde wrote his most famous play, *The Importance Of Being Earnest,* in 1894. He was staying in Worthing during the summer of that year to escape his creditors in London, being inspired to write the play by an article in the *Worthing Gazette* about a baby found in a hamper on Kings Cross Station. It took him just 21 days to write the play, the hero of which he named John Worthing in honour of the town. Two miles to the west of Worthing is Goring-by-Sea, where in a house called Sea View the naturalist Richard Jefferies lived out his last few months. The house has been named Jefferies House in his honour.

TOP TEN WINDMILLS IN SUSSEX

Argos Hill, *near Mayfield, East Sussex*
Built on an old-established mill site, Argos Hill is a fine example of a post mill, and is believed to date from 1835. It was worked by the Westons, a milling family, continuously until 1912/1913, and ceased to be worked in 1927. Subsequently the local district council assumed responsibility for its upkeep and it enjoyed extensive renovation during the 1960's and 1970's, including replacement of its sweeps. It is noteworthy for its splendid setting high up in the Sussex Weald, on a hill 605 ft above sea level.

Chailey, *near Lewes, East Sussex*
Chailey windmill is actually situated at North Common, close to Chailey Heritage, a special school that was established for handicapped children in 1903. A smock mill, it was built in 1830 and stands at the approximate centre of Sussex on what is now Chailey Common Nature Reserve. In 1844 it was transported to Newhaven, but it was subsequently brought back to Chailey in 1864 and continued to be worked until 1911. It was decapitated in 1928 as a result of a gale but was rebuilt by Neves millwrights in 1933 only for another storm to break the windshaft just 2 years later! Once again Neves came to the rescue and the mill was restored; it remains an important landmark to this day.

Clayton, *near Burgess Hill, West Sussex, 01273 843263*
Two windmills for the price of one! These are the famous Jack and Jill windmills, superbly situated on the South Downs escarpment and just a short walk from the South Downs Way National Trail. Jack is a black-painted tower mill that was built in 1866 to replace another mill on this site. Jill is a smaller wooden post mill that was built in about 1821 and originally sited in Dyke Road, Brighton, but was in 1852 towed to its present spot by a team of oxen. Both continued working until the first decade of the 20th century, and although Jack is now part of a private house once lived in by the famous golf commentator and writer Henry Longhurst, Jill has been restored to working condition and in modern times has seen flour being ground once again.

Halnaker, *near Chichester, West Sussex*
Halnaker Windmill is a brick tower mill standing on Halnaker Hill above Halnaker village about three miles east of Chichester. Built in around 1750 on the site of at least one earlier mill, it is one of the oldest windmills in existence, with walls that are 4 ft thick. It was restored first in 1934 and again in 1955. It ceased working in 1900 and the sails were blown down in 1913, so fresh sails were needed in the restoration process. During World War 2 it was used as an observation post and a navigational aid for aircraft, and in 1958 responsibility for the mill was assumed by the county council. It is certainly one of the most spectacularly situated windmills in the country, occupying a superb hilltop position and visible for miles around, with

tremendous views from the mill across vast swathes of Sussex countryside and out to sea. *Ha'nacker Mill* is the title of a poem by Hilaire Belloc who himself owned a mill elsewhere in Sussex.

High Salvington, *near Worthing, West Sussex, tel 01903 262443*

High Salvington Windmill was built at the start of the 18th century, and it is thought that this was the first windmill in England to be insured against fire. It is the last surviving example of a "post and socket" mill, a type of mill that was common from that late medieval period. Such mills consisted of a weighty cross-shaped base with a hefty central upright round which the mill's sails and timber superstructure could pivot; the central post of High Salvington Windmill was believed to be an oak tree. It was last worked during the First World War, and although it was kept in good order for a while afterwards, its condition deteriorated after the Second World War. However some really splendid restoration work has since been done, making it a popular visitor attraction.

Medmerry, *near Selsey, West Sussex*

The windmill at Medmerry stands closer to the sea than any other windmill in the Top Ten – just 200 yards, in fact. A converted red-brick tower mill, it was built in around 1805 and for virtually all of the 19th century it was used for grinding for flour and feeds. In the early 1890's this work ceased and the mill fell into disrepair, but in 1907/8 the tower was gutted and it was rebuilt as a 4-floor grist mill. Towards the end of its working life, the business which kept it going was the grinding of peppercorns. It ceased working in the 1920's but has now taken on a new lease of life as a holiday attraction, being part of the large West Sands leisure complex on the outskirts of Selsey, and in the holiday season it is even illuminated at night!

Nutley, *near Uckfield, East Sussex*

The windmill at Nutley is perhaps the oldest post mill standing in Sussex today. There is evidence that it dates back to 1817, although the first official record of its existence was not made until 1840. A number of different families had possession of the mill during its working life; its last miller was William Taylor, who milled here from 1874 until it ceased to work in about 1908 following failure to the structure of the body of the mill. Saved from collapse and renovated in 1928, it was workable once again by 1972 following extensive restoration (it had reached near collapse once more by 1969). The Uckfield Preservation Society were in 1984 given a European Heritage Award for its work in restoring the mill.

Polegate, *East Sussex*

A tower mill built in 1817 by a Mr Joseph Seymour, it stayed in the Seymour family for about 40 years. Grinding through wind power continued right up to the Second

World War, then after the war it continued to work, now powered by electric motor, right through to 1965. It had become quite run down, but was saved by the Eastbourne & District Preservation Trust and nearly all the machinery survives. Today it is the only tower mill in Sussex that is open to the public, and it also houses a fascinating museum with many exhibits and photographs of Sussex milling and a fine working model of a Sussex post mill. The only thing that lets Polegate windmill down is its rather undistinguished suburban setting.

Polegate Windmill.

***Shipley,

near Horsham, West Sussex, tel 01403 730439

The most impressive windmill in Sussex as well as one of the tallest, this is known as King's Mill; from the ground to the tip of the sails is nearly 100 ft. It was built in 1879 at a cost of £2500, built by a firm of Horsham millwrights and engineers with the very appropriate name of Grist and Steele. It was the last smock mill – ie a mill having top floors of wood, as opposed to a tower mill with brick-built top floors – to be built in Sussex, and it was also the biggest. The mill was purchased by the writer Hilaire Belloc in 1906 and ceased working in 1926 at the request of its owner because he found the mill traffic past his nearby study window to be a distraction! However, the mill is not only now frequently open to visitors, but when open can be put to work as well: to quote Spence, "On certain summer weekends....the great sweeps turn, sacks of wheat rise gently on the hoist to the top of the mill, and the grain drops through the shoots to the grindstones, then down the meal shoots to the bins below." Even if closed to the public, the mill itself is a magnificent spectacle, soaring up above the surrounding fields and visible for miles.

West Blatchington, *Hove*

This smock mill was recorded by Pevsner as dating from the 1720's, but subsequent research suggests it was built a full century later. Formerly part of the buildings of Blatchington Farm, it rose out of an L-shaped barn in which was the machinery driven by the mill. It was used for grinding flour and feed until it ceased working in around 1897 or 1898. Restoration began about forty years later, after it had been acquired by the local authority. Described by Pevsner as an "eminently curious piece," the mill is now surrounded by suburban housing but is still a prominent landmark even today.

West Blatchington windmill.

TOP TEN VIEWPOINTS IN SUSSEX

***Beachy Head, *near Eastbourne, East Sussex*
Large car park beside well-signposted road off A259 Eastbourne-Seaford road. Unparalleled views eastwards to Eastbourne and Hastings, and westwards to Brighton and beyond, as well as miles of intervening countryside and coastline; on a clear day it is claimed that Dungeness, the Isle of Wight and even the north coast of France can be made out.

Beacon Hill, *near South Harting, West Sussex*
Car park off Chichester-South Harting road at top of Harting Hill; follow South Downs Way eastwards and detour steeply uphill to summit. Great views to Chichester Harbour and parts of the Portsmouth conurbation, the Isle of Wight, the South Downs escarpment looking east, and the Weald.

Chanctonbury Ring, *near Washington, West Sussex*
Small car park just off road leading uphill southwards from Washington on to A24. Follow South Downs Way to just short of Ring itself. Tremendous views to the Weald, the sea, the coastal towns of Littlehampton and Worthing, and the South Downs escarpment to the west.

Devil's Dyke, *near Hove*
Car park by the Dyke. From a small ridge beside the trig point immediately to the west of the car park across a field. Magnificent views to the Weald, the South Downs escarpment back to Chanctonbury, and a broad swathe of coastline including Brighton, Shoreham and Worthing. It may be possible to identify the Isle of Wight in exceptionally clear conditions.

Devil's Humps, *Kingley Vale Nature Reserve, near Chichester*
Car park by West Stoke Church, 45-50 min walk through the Reserve. Wonderful grandstand view of Channel coast, Chichester Cathedral, Harbour and surrounding countryside, and, to the north, miles of beautiful unspoilt downland, rolling hills and woodlands.

Ditchling Beacon, *near Ditchling*
Small car park immediately off Ditchling-Brighton road at summit. The easiest viewpoint for the motorist to enjoy, with a magnificent view across a huge area of Wealden countryside, but there are also fine views towards the coast between Newhaven and Seaford. One of the highest points on the South Downs at just over 800 ft.

Firle Beacon, *near Firle*
Car park at end of road leading southwards off A27 signposted Firle, follow South Downs Way for just under a mile eastwards to trig point. A superb viewpoint including

the towns of Lewes, Newhaven, Seaford and Polegate, a large portion of coastline, the Ouse valley, and a large area of Wealden countryside.

Kithurst Hill, *near Storrington, West Sussex*
Car park at south end of Chantry Lane; quarter of a mile walk westwards along South Downs Way then short walk northwards to hilltop along marked path. Lovely views to the Weald, the Arun valley including Arundel Castle, and a broad sweep of coast including Bognor Regis, Littlehampton and Worthing.

Toby Stone, *near Bignor, West Sussex*
Car park at top of Bignor Hill; half-mile walk eastwards along South Downs Way Magnificent views to the sea, countryside around Chichester, the Weald, the Arun valley, South Downs escarpment eastwards towards Rackham Hill and Chanctonbury Ring.

Windover Hill, *near Alfriston, East Sussex*
Small car park at brow of hill on Wilmington-Lullington road, follow South Downs Way (bridle route) eastwards then detour uphill to trig point. A superbly diverse landscape encompassing the coastline around Seaford Head and the Seven Sisters, the South Downs escarpment towards Firle Beacon, a large area of Weald and the suburbs of Eastbourne.

TOP TEN DISASTERS IN SUSSEX

Shipwreck of La Nympha Americana, 29th November 1747: La Nympha Americana was a cargo ship weighing 800 tons and at the time was travelling through the English Channel bearing a variety of goods including precious clothes, £5000 in cash and £30,000 worth of quicksilver. The ship was caught in galeforce winds and violent snowstorms off Beachy Head; its bottom was ripped out while its superstructure was hurled on to the base of the cliffs at Birling Gap. At least 100 sailors were killed.

Great Convoy Disaster, 7th December 1809: The convoy in question, led by the 186-ton sloop HMS Harlequin, was deputed for the purpose of protecting small trading craft from French attack. As it travelled through the Channel it encountered severe weather. The Harlequin ran aground on a steep shingle bank of longshore drift at Seaford, and the whole convoy quickly disintegrated. Described as a "calamitous multiple stranding," the disaster claimed 31 lives.

Lewes avalanche, 24th December 1836: It had been snowing for days with accompanying gales which created deep drifts. The violence of the gale deposited a continuous ridge of snow along the brow of the heights based by South Street and Eastbourne Road. On Christmas Eve, a great mass of snow cascaded on to houses below, breaking over them and dashing them on to the road. Fifteen people were buried under many tons of snow and eight lost their lives.

Collapse of Chichester Cathedral Spire, 21st February 1861: At the time, the cathedral was undergoing restoration and enlargement. As a result of a gale, the piers gradually gave way allowing the tower and spire to sink eerily into the nave. At the time, the loss of this landmark of national importance was greeted with a mixture of grief and incredulity.

Clayton Tunnel Rail Crash, 25th August 1861: A tunnel signalling error resulted in a horrendous crash involving three trains. Many of the passengers were day trippers on their way back to London from Brighton. Some of the bodies were maimed and mangled out of all recognition. A total of 22 passengers lost their lives, and nearly 200 were injured.

Handcross Bus Crash, 12th July 1906: On this summer day a Vanguard bus was carrying 34 men from the St Mary Cray & Orpington Fire Brigade on an excursion to Sussex. In the village of Handcross the driver lost control of the bus which collided with an oak tree. The top deck of the bus was sliced off and bodies were hurled like children's toys through the plateglass windows. The inquest blamed the driver for the accident, which claimed 10 lives.

Rye Lifeboat Disaster, 1928: Gales were gusting up to 80mph in the Channel when the Rye lifeboat crew were called out in the Mary Stanford to rescue the Latvian ship Alice. By a supreme irony the crew of Alice were saved by another ship, but the violent seas caused the Mary Stanford to capsize. 17 lifeboatmen lost their lives in what was the worst British lifeboat disaster for over 40 years. A memorial to the dead stands in the churchyard at Rye Harbour.

***Bombing of Petworth Boys School, 29th September 1942: Although many Sussex people lost their lives or their homes through bombing in World War 2, this is regarded as the most tragic and destructive bombing incident in Sussex. On a late September day in 1942 a low-flying Junkers 88 bombed Petworth Boys School. The school was flattened and the result was what is described as "a scene of carnage (and) utter desolation." 28 schoolboys and 2 teachers were killed.

Blackdown Air Crash, 4th November 1967: On this day a Caravelle plane belonging to Iberian Airlines and travelling from Malaga to Heathrow crashed into the slopes of Blackdown Hill. All 7 crew and 30 passengers were killed instantly. The crash carved a corridor of devastation 400 metres wide. Beech trees were reduced to matchsticks, over a hundred sheep were killed, and the bodies of the people who perished were so badly mangled in the wreckage as to be unrecognisable.

Destruction of Uppark by fire, 30th August 1989: This magnificent National Trust property near South Harting in West Sussex caught fire one warm, windy late summer afternoon. The fire quickly spread and at one time 157 firemen from across three counties were involved in fighting it. Though many of the house's priceless treasures were saved, the loss and damage was colossal. At first it was believed that the house had been gutted; in fact this was not the case, but the cost of restoring the house came to around £20 million.

TOP TEN PLACES TO WATCH BIRDS IN SUSSEX

Beachy Head, *near Eastbourne, East Sussex*
One of the best known beauty spots in Southern England and the highest chalk sea cliffs in Britain, Beachy Head offers an impressive range of birds seen adjacent to and on the cliffs. Residents include the herring gull and jackdaw, and among nearly 40 visiting species in autumn is the honey buzzard. Best time to visit: autumn.

Bewl Water, *near Flimwell, East Sussex (best base: information centre at end of road leading to the water off A21 Flimwell-Lamberhurst road)*
Set in an area of outstanding natural beauty in the heart of the High Weald with a wide range of habitats, over 200 species of birds have been recorded to date. Residents include tawny owl, treecreeper and nuthatch. Best time to visit: autumn.

Burton Pond, *Petworth, West Sussex (off A285 just south of Petworth)*
A mosaic of different habitats makes Burton Pond, together with its neighbour Chingford Pond, a very rewarding place to explore with the likelihood of seeing a wide variety of birds on a comparatively short walk. Residents include gadwall, treecreeper, and marsh and coal tits. Best time to visit: late winter/spring.

Chichester Harbour, *West Sussex (best base: Thorney Island looking out to Pilsey Island which boasts an RSPB reserve)*
The harbour is of international importance for its wetland landscape and a site of Special Scientific Interest. Residents include the grey heron, black-tailed godwit and curlew, and among well over 45 visiting species in winter are the peregrine and guillemot. Best time to visit: winter.

Cuckmere Valley, *Seaford, East Sussex (best base: Exceat Bridge on A259 Seaford-Eastbourne road)*
The Cuckmere Valley is designated an Area Of Outstanding Natural Beauty and a site of Special Scientific Interest. Residents include the kingfisher, little egret and ringed plover, and among well over 40 visiting species in spring include the red-breasted merganser and eider. Best time to visit: spring.

Kingley Vale, *Chichester, West Sussex (best base: main car park by West Stoke Church)*
Kingley Vale is a nature reserve of breathtaking beauty and variety, and it is said that there are few better places in the county to hear the dawn chorus. Residents include the common buzzard, kestrel and great spotted woodpecker. The reserve is best visited in the spring and summer when the diversity of birds is at its greatest.

***Pagham Harbour, *near Bognor Regis, West Sussex (best base: information centre on left of B2145 travelling south from Sidlesham towards Selsey)*
The harbour boasts an excellent range of habitats and birds and is regarded as one of

the most popular destinations for birdwatchers. Residents include the mute swan and skylark, and among over 40 visiting species in winter are the cormorant, dunlin and wigeon. Best time to visit: winter.

Pevensey Levels, *near Pevensey, East Sussex (best base: Star Inn, Normans Bay off A259)*
This large area is underwatched and can provide very rewarding birdwatching at any time of year. August 1993 saw only Britain's fourth oriental pratincole on Pevensey Levels. Residents include the Canada goose and meadow pipit, while winter, the best time to visit, may include sightings of a Bewick's swan or fieldfare.

Pagham Harbour: a paradise for birdwatchers and a lovely place to walk and relax.

Rye Bay, *Rye, East Sussex (best base: Terney Pool reached by path from Rye Harbour village)*
Rye Harbour local nature reserve has been recognised as a special protection area for birds; in April 2003 the county's first ever Pacific golden plover was sighted here. Residents include the shelduck and linnet, while in the winter, the best time to visit., there are around 40 regular visitors including the bittern and merlin.

Selsey Bill, *Selsey, West Sussex (Best base: seaward side of the garden of Bill House, a former coastguard tower)*
This is regarded as one of the best places in Sussex to observe seabird movements in the English Channel. Residents include the little grebe, barn owl and yellowhammer while the spring, the best time to visit, brings sightings of the whimbrel and great skua.

TOP TEN NON-SPORTING EVENTS IN SUSSEX

Airborne.

Airbourne, *Eastbourne, East Sussex*

This is the annual airshow held at Eastbourne; in 2005 it celebrated its 13th year and in 2004 it attracted 800,000 visitors. It is particularly noteworthy for its spectacular flying displays which can be viewed from a number of vantage points such as the slopes of the South Downs towards Beachy Head, the Wish Tower Slopes, the Pier, the Promenade and beaches. In 2004 the world famous Red Arrows flew on three of the four days.

Birdman Rally, *Bognor Regis, West Sussex*

This annual competition to see how far a human being can fly had its origins in 1971 at nearby Selsey, where it continued successfully until 1977. By 1978 the event had become so big that it was moved to its current location at Bognor Regis Pier and has now become a huge media spectacle, as large numbers of competitors attempt to fly from the pier end, watched by upwards of 30,000. The record flight now stands at 89.2 metres, achieved in 1992.

***Brighton Festival

One of the biggest arts festivals in the country, with attendances topping 430,000 in 2004. There is a vast number of events packed into the 3-week festival which takes place annually in May, from traditional theatre, opera and dance to experimental music and drama, from guest appearances of top celebrities to fringe events, debates, quizzes, family fun days and exhibitions. Guests in 2005 included David Frost, Janet Street-Porter and Roy Hattersley, and there were performances from the London Symphony Orchestra and English National Opera.

Chichester Festivities

Perhaps the most prestigious arts festival in Sussex outside Brighton, the Chichester Festivities are held early in July each year and pack a huge amount of activity into this small city. The Cathedral hosts many of the top events which in 2005 included performances by Dame Felicity Lott, the Tallis Scholars, Humphrey Lyttleton and his band, and Rolf Harris and his band. Guest speakers in the Festivities in 2005 included the explorer Pen Hadow, Sir Max Hastings and Sheila Hancock, and there are numerous concerts, talks, exhibitions and guided walks.

The Chichester Festival Theatre continues to attract world-famous actors and performers and is one of the main focal points of the Chichester Festivities each summer.

Lewes Bonfire Night, *Lewes, East Sussex*

It is at Lewes that arguably the largest and most famous annual bonfire celebration is held. Traditionally, the evening's events have begun with the lighting of torches and then a torchlit procession involving a march of up to 3000 "Bonfire Boys and Girls" watched by up to 60,000 spectators; following the procession, bonfires have been lit and there has been a massive display of glittering fireworks. The most controversial aspect of the celebrations has been the burning of Papal effigies, a custom stemming from the suggestion that the original Gunpowder Plot was initiated by Pope Pius IV.

London to Brighton Bike Ride

This event, organised by the British Heart Foundation, started in 1980 and is held each June. Since its inception, the event has raised more than £26 million for the charity and has attracted more than 550,000 riders; it is the Heart Foundation's biggest fundraising event of the year as well as the biggest bike ride in Europe, and it is so popular that applications from thousands of cyclists to take part have to be turned down to prevent overcrowding on the roads, some roads are now shut to motorists to allow the passage of bikes, and in 2005 bikes were banned from local train services on the day of the ride!

London to Brighton Bike Ride.

London to Brighton Veteran Car Run

The 2004 event was the 71st running of this world famous event spanning 108 years. Nearly 500 cars now take part: in 2004 they included an 1896 Arnold Dogcart that took part in the original 1896 event, plus a 1901 Mors, a 1902 Napier and a 1903 De Dion Bouton. Held on the first Sunday in November, it is the world's longest running motoring event and one of the most testing veteran car endurance events, attracting thousands of spectators.

Pride Festival, *Brighton*

Pride in Brighton and Hove is a charitable trust serving the Gay, Lesbian, Bisexual and Transgender community of Brighton and Hove and surrounding areas. It organises two Pride Festivals, one in February and one in August. Both are a week long series of community events, of which the more popular is the Summer Festival. This culminates with a Carnival Parade and a day long free event in Preston Park. In 2004 this event attracted over 100,000 visitors and contributed more than £3.13m to the local economy.

RAF Association Airshow, *Shoreham Airport, West Sussex*

This annual show takes place in early September, and is described as one of the best airshows in the UK. Run by volunteers with all proceeds going to the Royal Air Forces

Association, the event has raised almost £900,000 up to 2004. The 2005 event celebrated the 60th anniversary of VE and VJ Day, and included flying displays with full commentary, a chance to meet the pilots, a classic car and motor show, an opportunity to ride in a helicopter, and a large static aircraft display.

South of England Show, *South of England Centre, Ardingly, West Sussex*
This is the flagship event of the South of England Agricultural Society, held each June. It is the most popular outdoor agricultural event in the South East, and includes displays of prize-winning British cattle, pigs, sheep and goats, international show jumping, daily cattle and livestock events, driving displays provided by the Hackney Horse Society, an equestrian relay competition, various countryside demonstrations and displays, floral displays, a food fair and band music.

TOP TEN SPORTING VENUES IN SUSSEX

Brighton Racecourse, *Brighton, tel 01273 603580*
Located on the outskirts of Brighton with spectacular views to the Sussex Downs and Brighton Marina, the racecourse holds over 20 meetings a year including the prestigious John Smiths Brighton Mile, and holds numerous other public events.

Cowdray Park Polo Club, *Midhurst, West Sussex, tel 01730 813257*
One of the best known polo venues in the country, the club hosts numerous prestigious polo events yearly including the British Open Championship for the Veuve Cliquot Gold Cup in June and July, and the British Ladies Championship in September. The setting, close to the Cowdray Ruins, is magnificent.

Devonshire Park, *Eastbourne, East Sussex, tel 01323 415442*
This is the venue for the annual pre-Wimbledon ladies tennis tournament on the WTA tour featuring some of the world's top ten ladies tennis players. Other major tennis tournaments are held here during the summer.

East Sussex National Golf Club, *Uckfield, East Sussex, tel 01825 880088*
There are two Championship golf courses here, the East and the West course. The East course is a 7138 yard stadium layout designed for tournament play. It has been the setting for many important tournaments including the European Open on two occasions. The golf offered here is said to be "the nearest you can get to perfection in the design and condition of golf courses."

Fontwell Park Racecourse, *near Arundel, West Sussex, tel 01243 543335*
With its friendly atmosphere and excellent viewing, this has been voted by the Racegoers Club as the Best Small Racecourse In The South East for the past 12 years. The mile-long steeplechase course hosts a number of meetings each year with some in 2005 combining racing with other activity such as family entertainment, charity fund raising, and performances from tribute bands.

***Goodwood, *Chichester, West Sussex, tel 01243 755000*
Goodwood could be regarded as the sporting mecca of Sussex. Its racecourse, with its fantastic hilltop setting, holds the famous Glorious Goodwood event every July as well as numerous other race meetings during the year; the Festival of Speed, in the grounds of Goodwood House, is now a key event in the motor sport calendar; the Goodwood Revival meeting on a circuit adjacent to Goodwood House, is a 3 day historic race meeting for the kind of motorcycles that would have competed at Goodwood during 1948-66; and there is also a fine golf course.

The main stand at Goodwood racecourse bathed in hot summer sunshine on a non-racing day.

Hickstead All England Jumping Course, *Hickstead, West Sussex, tel 01273 834315*
The course was created by one Douglas Bunn "to put on the best show jumping possible at a venue that is superior to anything found in the world." It is now regarded as the home of international show jumping in Great Britain, hosting numerous world class events; almost every great show jumper, horse and rider since 1960 has competed here.

Hove Cricket Ground, *Hove, 01273 827100*
The headquarters of Sussex County Cricket Club, county Champions for the first time in 2003, this ground has hosted county cricket since 1872 and seen some of the finest cricketers in the world set foot on its turf.

Plumpton Racecourse, *near Lewes, East Sussex, tel 01273 890383*
Set against a wonderful South Downs backdrop, this is one of the most successful smaller jump racecourses in the country, staging 16 National Hunt fixtures a year from September to May.

Withdean, *Brighton, tel 01273 776992*
This has been the home ground of Brighton and Hove Albion Football Club since 1999. Originally built as a venue for Davis Cup tennis in the 1930's, it has also hosted athletics and American Football events and holds 7000 supporters, all seated. The first Football League match played here in 1999 saw Brighton beat Mansfield 6-0.

TOP TEN COUNTRY CHURCHES IN SUSSEX

St Wilfrid's Chapel, *Church Norton, Selsey, West Sussex:*
This church stands in a beautiful secluded churchyard within sight of the wonderfully picturesque Pagham Harbour. It is in fact the 13th century chancel of a large medieval church, the main part of which was removed to Selsey. There is a fine monument to John and Agnes Lewis, dating back to 1537, and there is some vivid carving depicting the martyrdom of St Agatha. The church also has strong connections with Rudyard Kipling, who wrote the splendid legend of the priest Eddi and the Christmas-tide service he conducted here attended only by animals.

Coombes, *near Steyning, West Sussex*
The setting of this church could hardly be more rural and one might wonder how the church came to be there at all: there is a suggestion that it might have been a hermit's cell. The church has a Norman interior divided by a simple chancel arch – the chancel is thought to date from about 1200 while the chancel arch and nave are early Norman – and the east window dates from the 16th century. Its chief treasure is its 12th century wall paintings of the Lewes Cluniac School. With many shades of red and yellow with black and white, the paintings depict humans and animals.

***St Andrew's, *Didling, Midhurst, West Sussex*
The rural setting of this church is described by Simon Jenkins as "incomparable" and its beautiful position at the foot of the Downs has given it the title of the Shepherds' Church. The font is the only remnant from the Saxon period, the rest dating from the early 13th century. Features of interest include remarkable old bench ends with holders for candles, early Gothic windows, and a rough-carved Jacobean pulpit, but what will strike many visitors the most is the church's amazingly timeless atmosphere.

Lullington, *Alfriston, East Sussex*
This is the smallest church in Sussex, with room for barely 20 worshippers. Dating from the 14th century, it is actually the chancel of what was a much larger building. It has a beautiful downland setting and an extraordinarily intimate feel. Pevsner remarks that it will "not easily be forgotten."

North Stoke, *near Amberley, West Sussex*
This spacious church, elegant yet unfussy, enjoys an idyllic rural setting in the shade of the South Downs, boasting what the

Lullington Church.

The isolated but exceedingly pretty St Michael's Church, Penhurst, near Battle, in summer sunshine.

Churches Conservation Trust describe as "a memorable combination of rustic charm, fine architecture and an atmosphere of centuries of prayer." It has been virtually unaltered since medieval times, and features of interest include traces of 14th century wall painting, very rare 14th century stained glass, impressive sedilia, some intriguing stone carving and, on the outside wall, a medieval mass dial.

St Michael's, *Penhurst, Battle, East Sussex*

This church has an outstanding setting, beside a lovely lane close to a remote junction of rural roads in rolling wooded countryside. Simon Jenkins describes it as "welcoming and warm, a charming discovery well off any beaten track." The interior has a timeless quality, with its old box pews, Jacobean pulpit, and roughly carved Perpendicular screen separating nave and chancel. Of particular note are two fine carved bench-end tops, or poppyheads, detached from their seats, in the north chapel.

Southease, *near Lewes, East Sussex*

This little chapel has a stunning setting at the end of a cul de sac beyond Rodmell above a village green with a tree-framed manor house behind; Norman in origin, the church's original chancel and aisles have gone although some Norman work remains. The most interesting feature is the 15th century chancel arch of wood, lath and plaster, while remains of Reformation texts can be made out between the arches. The church also boasts a Jacobean pulpit and three rows of box pews.

St Michael's, *Up Marden, Chichester, West Sussex*

This church is apparently Gothic in origin but, to quote Simon Jenkins, it "exists in a time and place of its own." Accessible only along a track beside a house, it is virtually devoid of architecture. There are thick walls and single lancet windows, there is a Victorian Gothic pulpit which Jenkins describes as "fussy," and the wooden benches and box pews are said by Jenkins to be a "study in tranquillity." The setting, in a quiet hillside village surrounded by glorious countryside, is miraculous.

The Holy Sepulchre, *Warminghurst, Storrington, West Sussex*
This now redundant church sits on a hillside overlooking the South Downs, with Chanctonbury Ring close by. It has an early Gothic exterior and an interior which appears dominated by the Queen Anne screen dividing nave and chancel, composed of 3 classical arches and with Queen Anne's coat of arms painted above them. The church also boasts a fine arched roof, and 18th century pinewood box pews. Simon Jenkins remarks that the clerk's Elmwood chair beneath the pulpit "was plainly tailor-made for a vast posterior."

St George's, *West Grinstead, Horsham, West Sussex*
This church has a beautiful setting on the banks of the river Adur, its shingled spire a conspicuous landmark in the surrounding meadows. The architecture is described by Simon Jenkins as a "rustic jumble;" in the middle of the south aisle is the base of what must have been a huge Norman tower, while the nave arcade in the south aisle is more modest with three Early Gothic arches. There are some striking memorials including a 1746 monument to the Powletts, showing a man and wife in Roman dress leaning on an urn before an obelisk. Another most interesting feature is the naming of local farms on the pew backs.

The tiny country church of St Michael's, Up Marden, high up on the Downs in remote countryside between Chichester and Petersfield.

The Theatre Royal in Brighton, home of the Grey Lady, one of the more infamous ghosts in Sussex.

TOP TEN GHOSTS IN SUSSEX

A Lady in Blue at Alfriston appeared to a woman who was washing up in a back kitchen of Deans Place Hotel. She felt a gentle tap and saw a beautiful lady in a bright blue silk dress who then suddenly vanished. Another ghost local to Alfriston was the heir to the Chowne Estate who when out for an evening stroll was ambushed and killed by a gang of rogues and who with his dog was said to reappear in ghostly form every 7 years.

Lady Webster's vision at Battle Abbey is said by Augustus Hare to have been of an old woman of terrifying appearance gazing at her when she drew back the curtains of her four-poster bed. She was so solid looking and her appearance so vivid that Lady Webster could even in her old age recall details of the ghost's clothing. Battle Abbey has seen other ghosts, including a monk spotted one evening gliding along the pavement towards the Abbey gateway. Some say the ghost of King Harold, who perished here, still lingers and in 1972 near the Chapter House a young boy had a vision of a man holding a long sword.

Martha of Brede was a young servant girl at Brede Place who lived in the reign of Henry VIII. She was hanged as a thief but had been happy in a nearby dell when alive, and this is where her ghost is said to have dwelt after her death. One Clare Sheridan recalls standing on a hill behind the house and felt the sensation of someone trying to push her away. The chapel of Brede Place is haunted by a ghost priest named John but his influence is felt to be wholly beneficial. Brede is said to have been the home of Old Oxenbridge, nicknamed the Ogre of Brede because he liked to eat children. It is said the children doped him and sawed him in half, and Groaning Bridge hereabouts is said to be haunted by a giant in the form of a sawn tree trunk.

The Grey Lady of the Theatre Royal, Brighton, is so-called because of her old-fashioned grey dress. She has been seen in the vicinity of no 1 dressing room by two former staff members, and elsewhere in the building by lighting technicians. She once tapped the actor Martin Jarvis on the shoulder and in 1982 she was seen by the actor Gerald Flood's wife, Anne, who heard a door banging and on opening it saw the Grey Lady for about a minute. Next to the Theatre Royal there used to be a restaurant called Il Teatro where in October 1979 it is reported that a knife mysteriously flew through the air, narrowly missing the manager's daughter.

***Old Strike-a-Light is arguably the most infamous of all Sussex ghosts. Around 1765 a fisherman by the name of Jervoise was arriving in Brighton with a catch of herring when he saw dazzling shafts of light from the Rising Sun Inn at the south end of this street. He banged on the door and the massive form of a ghostly man nicknamed Old Strike-a-Light appeared in front if him. Jervoise went to the inn to recover, only for the ghost to come and stand a few feet behind him. Jervoise slumped to the floor in a faint and never recovered consciousness.

Geranium Jane of Cuckfield was a servant of the King's Head pub in the village. She was seduced by her employer and fell pregnant by him. His lover, disenchanted with her and fearful of the consequences for him, killed her by dropping a vase of geraniums on her head. It is said that if any regular drinker at the pub has an affair, Geranium Jane gets upset; she shakes the offender's bed and causes the bedroom temperature to plummet. It is said that children playing upstairs in the building saw a ghostly woman with make-up streaming down her face. At nearby Cuckfield Park the resentful ghost of Mrs Ann Sergison, deprived of what she believed to be her right to ownershop of the Park, is said to swing on the oak entrance gates.

The bowler of Hangleton Manor was heard by the Hardwick brothers who until they left the manor in 1914 used to hear a heavily booted man trampling about, and in the Long Gallery they could hear heavy wooden balls and the scattering of skittles. Hangleton Manor also boasts a much more tragic ghost, that of a young servant girl who having given birth hurled her baby to its death. It is said that her ghost haunts the manor in an endless search for her child, and her ghostly figure manifests itself as a pair of white hands.

Major Vallance of Brooker Hall, Hove, died suddenly at the age of 46, and his eldest son was killed 6 years later. The house had actually been built for the Major. Since the sudden deaths of the Major and his son, witnesses have reported strange goings on in the Hall: objects moving around, footsteps heard when nobody was present inside, strange vibrations and unexplained coldness in the curator's room, a friend of the caretaker's daughter woken by someone tucking her in bed, and a painter who felt someone pinching his bottom.

The ghostly drummer of Herstmonceux was a huge figure, 9ft tall, who was said to march along the battlements of the castle with sparks flying from his drumsticks. Though there is a suggestion that this drummer was an invention designed to deter intruders, there are said to be two other ghosts stalking the castle. The first was Grace Pelham, sometime heiress to the castle who died of starvation in her 21st year, and known as the Grey Lady. The second was Georgina Naylor, known as the White Lady because when seen walking in the grounds she is always wearing a long white cloak like the one she used to wear when she was alive in the late 18th century.

Brother Cantator of Rye was a monk with a beautiful voice. He fell in love with a girl named Amanda and eloped with her but was caught and walled up alive. He is supposed to have lost his sanity and then his life whilst walled up. His ghost returns to search for Amanda and there have been reports of sightings of the ghosts of both him and Amanda in the town; one witness says because of his madness the only sound he could make was a horrible gobbling noise.

TOP TEN BIZARRE PLACE NAMES IN SUSSEX

Batchelor's Bump, near Hastings, East Sussex, owes its origin to one John Bachelor, a Tudor landowner who lived hereabouts; the Bump may be a reference to a hillock on his property.

Blackboys, near Heathfield, East Sussex, is derived from Richard Blakeboy, whose home it was in 1398, although local tradition likes to derive the name from the "black boys" or charcoal handlers who after a day at the iron foundries would come to the inn here for a well earned drink.

Bopeep, near Alfriston, East Sussex, is believed to be derived from a turnpike keeper peeping through his window looking out for travellers along what is now the main A27 road.

Didling, near Midhurst, West Sussex, is derived from the name of the territory of a Saxon tribal group known as the Dyddelingas, or Dyddel's people. By 1260 the name had been shortened to Didelinge, and in 1545 the name appeared as Dedlinge. The present name certainly rolls off the tongue rather more easily.

Great Wigsell, Bodiam, East Sussex, is derived from "Wicg's Hill," recorded as Wiggesell around 1200, and Wiggesulle in 1339.

Hammerpot, near Arundel, West Sussex, is derived from the "pot" or slight hollow at Harmans or Harmars Farm nearby.

Harebeating, near Hailsham, East Sussex, is derived from the name of a tribal territory called the Herebeorhtingas – Herebeorht's people.

Open Winkins, near East Dean, West Sussex, is an area of woodland recorded as Winkingas around 1220, thought to be derived from "wincing," being a term for woodland of an irregular shape.

***Pease Pottage, near Crawley, West Sussex, was said to originate from days when prisoners under escort to Horsham Gaol were halted at a gate hereabouts and fed a dish of cold pottage, a mash of boiled dried peas. However there is no hard evidence to substantiate this and it is more than likely that the name is an allusion to the muddy condition of the local road.

Plonk Barn, near Alfriston, East Sussex, refers to a building constructed of "planke" or planks, and nothing to do with alcohol smuggling!

A tractor seems to be about to negotiate the extraordinary Byepass Bridge at Easebourne, near Midhurst.

TOP TEN BIZARRE LANDMARKS IN SUSSEX

Easebourne Private Byepass Bridge, *Easebourne, Midhurst, West Sussex*
Coming along the A272 Midhurst-Petworth road, one passes through the pretty village of Easebourne. Here on the north side one sees what looks like a small bridge erected for apparently no purpose. The sign explains all: "Private Byepass Bridge – Motors Not Exceeding 2 Tons May Use It At Own Risk – Dangerous And Forbidden To All Other Traffic." It was actually designed for horse traffic. Nowadays, even if the main carriageway is congested, it is hard to see what use any modern motorist or indeed horserider could make of it.

Long Furlong Tollhouse, *Clapham, near Worthing, West Sussex*
Tollhouses were nothing unusual, but this one, built in 1820 alongside what is now the busy A280 Clapham-Findon road, was particularly grand, having the appearance of a small castle, as though it ought to stand at the entrance to a huge mansion. However, no such mansion exists, and it remains an oddity albeit an aesthetically pleasant one to passing motorists.

***Long Man of Wilmington, *near Polegate, East Sussex*
The origin of this figure, carved into the South Downs above Wilmington, is a mystery. There is evidence to suggest it could date back to Saxon, Roman or even Bronze Age times, although it has been conceded that it might just be the work of an artistic monk from the nearby priory. Almost 250 ft high, and the largest such representation of a man in Europe, the Long Man still stands resplendently on the hillside, with what appears to be a staff in each hand.

Mad Jack's Pagoda, *Brightling, near Battle, East Sussex*
John Fuller, nicknamed Mad Jack, was a local squire, ironmaster and MP for East Sussex in the late 18th century who inherited a mansion at the pretty village of Brightling in 1777. Well known as an eccentric, he was best known for the follies he created around Brightling, possibly to relieve unemployment. The pagoda near his home in Brightling Park was designed by Sir Robert Smirke to house an observatory; it has two storeys and a lead-covered dome.

Mad Jack's Pyramid, *Brightling, near Battle, East Sussex*
Arguably John Fuller's best-known folly (see Mad Jack's Pagoda above) was the 60 ft high pyramid he had built in 1810 in the churchyard of Brightling church, still dwarfing most if not all of the other stones in the churchyard even today. Fuller was buried beneath the pyramid and legend asserts that he sits inside it, wearing a top hat and holding a bottle of claret.

Pepper Pot, *Tower Road, near Queens Park, Brighton*
This was designed by Sir Charles Barry, the architect of the House of Commons. It was

set in the grounds of a villa that was completed in 1830 and demolished in 1970, although the Pepper Pot remains. Used as an observation tower during World War 2, it is quite unclear why it was ever built in the first place! It now stands rather self-consciously at the end of a quiet residential street in the suburbs of Brighton.

Racton Tower, *near Westbourne, West Sussex*
This was built by the third Earl of Halifax in the early 1770's at a cost of about £10,000. His family home was at nearby Stansted House, and he built this tower as a lookout. The central tower rose up 80ft, with two smaller ones at the sides. Today the tower remains a prominent landmark, in a remote countryside setting, but with no possibility of access to the top, and no apparent plans to convert it into anything useful, it just looks rather pointless.

Sugar Loaf, *Woods Corner, Heathfield, East Sussex*
This odd building, which from a distance looks like the upper section of a church spire, stands about 40 ft high with walls 18 inches thick at the base, a narrow north-east facing entrance, and a single window due north. It is said that "Mad Jack" Fuller (see Mad Jack's Pyramid above) wanted to fool a guest at his house into thinking that he could see the spire of nearby Dallington Church from his home, and swiftly had this folly built as a replica on the basis that nobody could tell one from the other! In the late 19th century it was used as a 2-storey cottage for a farmer, and was restored in 1961 after being saved from demolition.

Toat Monument, *Pulborough, West Sussex*
This slim castellated octagonal hilltop tower in remote but beautiful countryside two miles north of Pulborough rises some 40ft high, and is a memorial to Samuel Drinkeld who died as a result of a fall from his horse in 1823. The tower was built four years later; it is remarkable that a comparatively unknown figure from the past should have such a prominent structure built in his honour. Sadly the tower itself is inaccessible to present day travellers.

Vandalian Tower, *Uppark, South Harting, West Sussex*
This was a Gothic folly built by Sir Matthew Fetherstonhaugh on Tower Hill near the big house at Uppark. Sir Matthew's son Harry inherited Uppark in 1774 and spent a great deal of time entertaining; his guests included George, Prince Regent. Sir Harry and his guests used to carouse in the 2-storey Vandalian Tower and it is said that their revelries were so excessive they had to be conveyed back to the house in wheelbarrows. The tower is now a ruin and stands on a hilltop looking somewhat abandoned with no hint of the excesses of yesteryear. It is inaccessible to visitors but can be viewed at fairly close range.

TOP TEN WEATHER EVENTS IN SUSSEX

On 4th February 1287, what was termed the "tempest of all tempests" changed the course of the river Rother, and what remained of old Winchelsea was utterly destroyed. The size and weight of the waves smashed down sea walls, swept away wooden buildings, and choked the river bed with shingle, sand and other debris, while all around was the wreckage of ships, inns, houses and churches.

***On 27th November 1703 there was arguably the worst storm in the history of Sussex. The wind began to blow at midnight and raged continuously for eight hours; across Britain, roughly 8000 people are thought to have been killed. In Brighton, 101 houses or shops in the lower town were destroyed by the wind or devoured by the sea. It was said that the coastal spray was driven so far inland that sheep declined to feed on the grass over an area of many miles.

On 20th May 1729 a tornado struck in Sussex. Although it lasted just 20 minutes, the damage was colossal. At Sidley Green, near Bexhill, the force of the wind moved a complete house off its foundations. Nearby, 150 oak trees were torn from their roots and shaken to pieces. The trail of devastation continued to Sedlescombe and on towards Tenterden, uprooting 1400 trees on the Battle Abbey estate.

During 1893 and 1895 Sussex experienced two severe droughts. Between 28th February and 3rd July 1893, Eastbourne recorded just 1.8 inches of rain, with only a few drops falling during a 60 day period starting from 17th March. The drought led to huge forest fires, and wells ran dry. Between 28th April and 17th July 1895, just two years later, just 0.68 inches of rain were recorded at Crowborough, and largely dry weather continued into 1896, with a loss of water of 1340 tons per acre across some areas.

The early months of 1963 saw the Big Freeze, with the coldest weather since 1740. The snow began on late afternoon of Boxing Day 1962, falling to a depth of 10 inches and creating massive drifts; 9 inches were cleared from Chichester alone. Near Wych Cross, in Ashdown Forest, 70 cars or lorries had to be dug from drifts. Between 26th and 31st December, 19 inches of snow fell at Horsham. The river Arun froze up in places, and at Eastbourne the sea froze for 100 ft off shore. At Weir Wood Reservoir a snow goose was spotted, this being the first sighting in the area since 1937. Food ran short, and postal deliveries had to be made by sledge. It was not all gloom: people enjoyed skiing on the downs, and skating on lakes and ponds.

1976 saw an exceptional summer. For 16 consecutive days during the summer, the temperature somewhere in England exceeded 90 degrees Fahrenheit. Sussex became tinder dry, with numerous fires. In June, Eastbourne recorded 323 hours of sunshine, an average of over 10 hours per day. Lack of rain created serious water supply problems, as reservoirs dried up and hosepipe bans were imposed.

1987 was the year of the Great Storm. October that year was extremely wet, and on the 7th of that month there was a mudslide at Rottingdean. Then in the early hours of the 16th, winds gusting at over 100mph swept across Sussex, claiming lives, destroying millions of trees and bringing down power lines. Church spires collapsed, blocks of flats had their roofs torn off, and at Bushy Hill 200 people on a caravan site ran for their lives as the wind devastated the caravans.

January 1994 saw the area to the north of Chichester deluged with flood water. Between 1st September 1993 and 1st January 1994, 600mm of rain fell in this area; the rainfall in December 1993 was nearly twice the average. By 12th January 1994 the river Lavant was flowing at 8 cubic metres per second compared with a normal January flow of 0.46. The culvert under Chichester city centre was unable to cope; properties and shops were flooded and there was widespread traffic chaos.

On 7th January 1998 Selsey was hit by a tornado. Amid a spell of very unsettled weather – just three days previously the town's defences had been severely tested by very high seas – this tornado struck shortly before midnight. It lasted just 30 seconds, but left 1000 homes damaged and a repair bill which was estimated to work out at £60,000 for every second of its duration. Miraculously nobody was killed or seriously injured.

In 2000 Lewes was very badly affected by flooding. Following days of incessant rain during October, the river Ouse in Lewes burst its banks, sweeping past the Tesco supermarket; then, to quote an eyewitness, "so much more water arrived so quickly. It overcame walls, rushed through gaps, and in minutes rather than hours the centre of the town was under water." The damage was extensive with several having to be rescued, and hundreds being evacuated; shops were inundated and stocks were ruined.

TOP TEN GARDENS IN SUSSEX

Borde Hill, *near Haywards Heath, West Sussex, tel 01444 450326*
One of the finest gardens for plant hunters in Sussex, this was created from 1893 with trees and shrubs collected from Europe, Asia, Tasmania and the Andes. The garden offers award-winning collections of azaleas, rhododendrons, magnolias and camellias as well as sub-Himalayan species, palms and bamboos; there are bluebell woods, extensive woodland walks, lakes and 220 acres of parkland.

***Great Dixter, *Northiam, near Rye, East Sussex, tel 01797 252878*
The house here was reinvented by Edwin Lutyens who enlarged it and designed the gardens. Striking features are the meadow garden, the colonies of bulbs, the orchard with its early purple orchids, the famous Long Border with a spectacular mixture of shrubs, climbers, perennials and annuals, a sheltered Exotic Garden which is a riot of tropical colours and unfamiliar shapes, and superb topiary on the approach to the High Garden with its "intriguing aesthetic melange" of plants and vegetables. It is said that "this is gardening with sheer joie-de-vivre."

Gardening with "sheer joie-de-vivre," one commentator writes: the amazing gardens and house at Great Dixter, Northiam, near Rye.

High Beeches, *Handcross, Crawley, West Sussex, tel 01444 400589*
This delightful garden, originally designed by Sir Edmund Loder in 1906, offers lovely walks meandering through wildflower meadows and past woodland and water, with a collection of rare trees and unusual shrubs. Alongside the National Collection of

stewartias are glades of rhododendrons, azaleas and magnolias, and the garden is continually extending its collection. Described as a "garden of many seasons," the garden offers superb spring bluebells, August gentian and autumn cyclamen, and a summerhouse and benches give the visitor the opportunity to enjoy the scents and colours at leisure.

Leonardslee, *Lower Beeding, near Horsham, West Sussex, tel 01403 891212*
This garden was enlarged by Sir Edmund Loder who raised the famous rhododendron "Loder" hybrids with huge scented flowers. The garden is set in a valley over 240 acres with seven lakes, mature trees, a collection of rhododendrons some of which are nearly 200 years old, azaleas, camellias and magnolias. There is a rock garden with ferns and Kurume azaleas, an excellent bonsai exhibition, and an alpine house with over 400 species of alpine plants.

Beautiful flowers and thick vegetation in springtime at Leonardslee, near Horsham.

Michelham Priory, *near Hailsham, East Sussex, tel 01323 844224*
Constructed on the moated site of an old priory, the garden is packed with colour and variety: exotic waterside plants, widely sweeping herbaceous border, fine ornamental "potager" with vegetables and flowers, physic garden, and a cloister

The gardens at Michelham Priory, near Polegate, are noted for their colour and variety; this is one corner of the gardens in early May.

garden inspired by illustrations of medieval Marian Gardens. The site also boasts a smithy, working watermill and rope museum.

Nymans, *Handcross, near Crawley, West Sussex, tel 01444 400321*
Started in 1890 by Ludwig Messel, this historic collection of fine trees, shrubs and plants in a beautifully structured setting is full of outstanding effects that are described as "almost theatrical," including sheets of white narcissi under sorbus trees, and a circle of camellias around a lawn. Nymans' other features include a sunken garden with stone loggia, a laurel walk, croquet lawn, heather garden, rose garden and magnificent herbaceous borders. The whole is exceptionally well maintained.

Pashley Manor, *Ticehurst, East Sussex, tel 01580 200888*
This Grade I listed Tudor timber-framed ironmaster's house has a formal garden which is noteworthy for its subtle planting and superb views. Visitors can enjoy a series of enclosed gardens with beautiful 18th century walls; grass paths lead through camellia and rhododendron shrubberies; and there are some good water features including natural springs and ponds, one of which includes a small island with classical temple.

Other features include magnificent hydrangeas, a garden of old-fashioned roses, ample herbaceous borders, and superb tulips in May.

Sheffield Park, *Lewes, East Sussex, tel 01825 790231*
This 120-acre landscape garden and arboretum with two lakes was created by Capability Brown for the Earl of Sheffield in 1776. Between 1909 and 1934 a collection of trees and shrubs were planted that were notable for their autumn colour, and these and other fine specimen trees provide all-year-round interest. The lakes boast fine water lilies, and in Queens Walk there is amazing colour to be found in the Chinese gentiana. The garden also has a number of recently rediscovered varieties of azaleas.

Wakehurst Place, *Ardingly, near Haywards Heath, West Sussex, tel 01444 894066*
The estate was bought in 1903 by Gerald Loder and developed by him over 33 years, and it has been managed by the Royal Botanical Gardens, Kew, since 1965. A mecca for the botanist, plantsman and garden lover alike, it is noteworthy for its fine collection of hardy plants, and there are four comprehensive national collections – betulas, hypericums, nothofagus and skimmias. One unique feature is its glade, planted with species growing at over 3000m in the Himalayas. There are fascinating water gardens including a plantation of Japanese irises, as well as two walled gardens and a Millennium seed bank that was opened in 2000.

West Dean, *Chichester, West Sussex, tel 01243 818210*
There have been gardens here since 1622. The gardens offer tremendous variety, with 35 acres of ornamental grounds, immaculately restored Victorian glasshouses with excellently labelled fruit and vegetables, an orchard containing a variety of fruit trees, potting sheds which house garden-themed exhibitions, a delightful sunken garden, jungle plants including bamboos and palms, a wild garden with unusual trees, the river Lavant which winds through the garden and is crossed by attractive bridges, and St Roche's Arboretum which is carpeted with wild daffodils in spring. The spring tulips are a particularly impressive feature.

TOP TEN GOLF COURSES IN SUSSEX

Crowborough Beacon, *Crowborough, East Sussex , tel 01892 661511*
This 6279 yd course is 800 ft above the sea, and is a testing heathland course with panoramic views of the South Downs; even Eastbourne can be seen on a clear day. The prospect from the first hole must be one of the finest from any opening hole in the country. Comments include: "Beautiful course with great views....a gem....heathland masteepiece."

East Sussex National, *Uckfield, East Sussex, tel 01825 880228*
There are in fact two courses here, the East at 7138 yds and the West at 7154 yds! They are huge courses, ideal for big hitters; the European Open has been staged here, and it is home to the European HQ of the David Leadbetter Golf Academy. The American-style courses with immaculately maintained greens are superbly designed and one visitor enthused "They treat you as though you have won the Lottery here."

Mannings Heath, *Horsham, West Sussex, tel 01403 210228*
There are two courses here, the Kingfisher and the Waterfall; the 6378 yd Waterfall is the Top Ten nominee, being a downhill, part parkland and part heathland championship course with streams and trees in abundance and three spectacular par 3's. The 10th and 11th are described as "fabulous back to back holes."

The Nevill, *near Frant, East Sussex, tel 01892 525818*
Designed by Henry Cotton, this 6349 yd course is on the border with Kent, very close to the Kent town of Tunbridge Wells. It is built on well-wooded, undulating open ground, with a mixture of heather and gorse on the front nine, while a feature of the back nine is a valley stream which presents a testing hazard on two holes. It is a well-established and most attractive course, and a fine test of golf.

Piltdown, *Uckfield, East Sussex, tel 01825 722033*
This charming and well designed 6076 yd course is a natural heathland course with much heather and gorse, offering easy walking, excellent greens and fine views, and although there are no bunkers it has been described as "brutal!"

Royal Ashdown Forest, *Forest Row, East Sussex, tel 01342 822018*
The Old Course is 6477 yds and lies on undulating heathland with no bunkers, offering magnificent views across Ashdown Forest. Ranked 94th in *Golf World's* most recent ranking of courses in the British Isles, it has a reputation for being the most demanding course in the South East with long carries off the tees and tight tree-lined fairways. It has been described as "just brilliant....a challenging, heathery, rugged course requiring great accuracy."

Rye, *East Sussex, tel 01797 225241*
This 6317 yd course is a unique links course with superb undulating greens, set among ridges of sand dunes alongside Rye Harbour with fine views towards Fairlight, Romney Marsh and Dungeness. Steeped in tradition, it offers classic links golf and has been described as "one of the most difficult courses around." NOTE: VISITORS MUST BE INVITED OR INTRODUCED BY A MEMBER.

Blatchington Golf Clubhouse.

Seaford, *East Blatchington, near Seaford, East Sussex, tel 01323 892442*
This 6551 yd course was originally designed by the great H Taylor, friend and rival of James Braid. It is a splendid downland course with magnificent views and some fine holes. Comments include "brilliant..... excellent views....tricky in the wind...finest inland course in the South."

***West Sussex Golf Club, *Pulborough, West Sussex, tel 01798 872563*
This 6223 yd course is an outstandingly beautiful heathland course occupying an oasis of sand, heather and pine in the middle of attractive countryside. Challenges exist on almost every hole with huge carries from the tee across vast expanses of deep purple heather. There is tremendous variety and excitement in the par 3's, including the 6th hole, a 200+ yard carry over a lake from an elevated tee, and the 15th hole, through a funnel of mature trees over a lake to a sloping green. Comments include: "You'll be hypnotised by its lush beauty.....tougher than it looks....kept in superb condition."

Worthing Lower Course, Links Road, Worthing, tel 01903 694664
This 6505 yd course is considered to be one of the best downland courses in the country, and has been described as very enjoyable as well as entertaining.

TOP TEN PUBS IN SUSSEX

(Sources: Which Pub Guide 2005, AA Pub Guide 2005 and The Good Pub Guide 2005)

The George and Dragon, *Burpham, near Arundel, West Sussex, tel 01903 883131*
There is just a small bar area here but most customers come to eat at this beautifully positioned village inn, very popular with overseas visitors, and offering super views to Arundel and its castle. There are well kept Arundel, Fullers, Harveys and Kings beers on handpump. Bar food includes scallops wrapped in bacon, seafood platter, steak and horseradish pie, and sticky toffee pudding. The bar has good strong wooden furnishings and lots of interesting prints, and there is a good wine list.

The Black Horse, *Byworth, near Petworth, West Sussex, tel 01798 342424*
This is a totally unspoilt pub in a beautiful garden. The interior dates back to the 14th century, and there are wooden floors and furniture, panelled walls and open fires. Good ales include Arundel Gold, Cheriton Pots Ale, Hogs Back Brew and Itchen Valley. Excellent food includes pheasant calvados, Cajun chicken, lasagne Verdi, crab cakes and steak and kidney pudding.

The Fox Goes Free, *Charlton, near Chichester, West Sussex, tel 01243 811461*
This is a cheerful, well-run country pub with low-beamed bar, old and new elm furniture, and huge brick fireplace with woodburning stove. Well kept Arundel Stronghold, Ballards Best, Fox Goes Free and Ringwoods Boondoggle are available on handpump, and several wines are available by the glass. Food includes honey roast ham with free range eggs, summer salads of warm chorizo, red onion and goats cheese and bacon, and baked American raspberry cheesecake.

The Cricketers, *Duncton, near Petworth, West Sussex, tel 01798 342473*
The bar has an open plan feel, and at one end is an inglenook fireplace with a good winter fire. Well-kept Youngs Bitter and a couple of guests from Ballards are available on handpump, and there are several good wines. There is a charming garden with lovely flower baskets and tubs at the front. Meals include sardine bruschetta, peppered beef, mushroom and Guinness pie, and fisherman's bag offers a variety of seafood delights including shellfish.

The Kings Arms, *Fernhurst, West Sussex, tel 01428 652005*
This Grade 2 listed 17th century free house and restaurant is blessed with dazzling hanging baskets, flowering tubs, vines and creepers. Its cooking style combines modern and traditional British recipes, with such delights as local butchers' sausage and mash, cod in beer batter, and roasted monkfish with basil ratatouille, while different fish specials are available almost every day. Beers include Kings Arms best bitter, Ringwood Brewery best bitter, Hogs Back and Caledonian.

The Halfway Bridge, *Lodsworth, Petworth, West Sussex, tel 01798 861281*
Three or four bar rooms can be found in this civilised comfortably furnished inn, with a nice bustling atmosphere. Well kept Cheriton Pots Ale, Gales HSB, Harveys Best and Kings Spring Ale are available on handpump, and the wine list is described as "thoughtful." Bar food includes rice and peanut cakes with spicy dipping sauce, sesame baked snapper with hot ginger marinade, mango rice pudding and walnut and treacle tart.

***The Gribble, *Oving, Chichester, West Sussex, tel 01243 786893*
This enormously popular 16th century thatched pub has its own-brewed real ales, including Gribble Ale, Pigs Ear, Plucking Pheasant, Regis Tipple, Slurping Stoat, Winter Wobbler and Badger Tanglefoot on handpump, and there are 20 country wines and farm cider. The several linked rooms give the pub a cottagey feel. Bar food includes ham and eggs, and red pepper and spinach lasagne. There is a pretty garden which contains apple and pear trees.

The Welldiggers, *Petworth, West Sussex, tel 01798 342287*
Good generous portions of fresh food can be found in this Thirties style ancient country pub. The smallish L-shaped bar has low beams, and from the bar can be obtained decent wines and well-kept Youngs on handpump. Food includes duck with apple sauce, salad nicoise, and vegetarian Wellington. There is no music or machines, and there are lovely views from the terrace.

The Horse and Groom, *Rushlake Green, Heathfield, East Sussex, tel 01435 830320*
This Grade 2 listed building on a vast village green offers beers including Harveys, Master Brew, and Shepherd Neame Spitfire. The food includes boiled knuckle of gammon with onion stock and butter beans, and there is an excellent fish choice including monkfish stuffed with chorizo on cherry brandy compote. The pub boasts a well-tended garden with shrubs, topiary, and little arches with climbers. The beams in the interior are described as seeming "blacker and thicker than most!"

The Mermaid, *Rye, East Sussex, tel 01797 223065*
This lovely black and white timbered inn on Rye's most picturesque street dates from Elizabethan times. A huge inglenook takes up almost an entire wall in the bar, and numerous ghost stories add to the appeal as do beams hewn from ancient ships' timbers, secret passages, and cosy log fires. Beers include Greene King Old Speckled Hen and Courage Best. Food includes moules mariniere, minute steak glazed with red onions, and seafood platter for two.

TOP TEN PLACES TO STAY IN SUSSEX

(Sources: AA Hotel Guide 2005, Good Hotel Guide 2005,
Which Guide to Good Hotels 2005)

***Amberley Castle,** Amberley, Arundel, West Sussex, tel 01798 831992*
This luxury hotel, set in immaculate gardens, is a treasure-trove of historical interest, including many fascinating original features such as an impressive gatehouse and portcullis. The day rooms are filled with antique furniture, while the individually decorated bedrooms, some boasting four poster beds and all containing spa baths, are charming; some even have direct access to the battlements and ramparts. Dining is a treat, with eclectic cooking which might include twice-baked stilton soufflé with spiced plum compote.

The Millstream, *Bosham, Chichester, West Sussex, tel 01243 573234*
This much-extended 18th century hotel in the heart of Bosham offers consistently excellent service. The bedrooms are immaculately kept, well equipped and individually decorated with pretty well-co-ordinated colours. Service has been described by one critic as "flawless." The hotel has a restaurant, bar, lounge and gardens.

Hotel du Vin, *Brighton, tel 01273 718588*
This tastefully-converted mock Tudor building is situated in a quiet side street close to the sea front. The individual bedrooms all have a wine theme and are comprehensively equipped, some en suite. The Penthouse Suite offers a private terrace, telescope and sea views. There is an atmospheric, locally popular restaurant with stylish modern décor including a black-painted vaulted ceiling. The food menu might include smoked organic salmon with cauliflower puree, and a good range of Mediterranean-style dishes.

Bailiffscourt, *Climping, Littlehampton, West Sussex, tel 01903 723511*
This medieval-looking manor does in fact date back to the 1920's but has been made to look like an ancient house. The bedrooms are spacious and atmospheric, beautifully stylish and luxuriously appointed with several four-posters. The recently-added outbuildings boast a good range of contemporary furnishings. There is a choice of cosy lounges with huge squishy sofas, and there is a well-equipped spa. The hotel is described as having a "thoroughly warm and inviting atmosphere."

Ockendon Manor, *Cuckfield, West Sussex, tel 01444 416111*
This 16th century hotel enjoys fine views of the South Downs and offers a very high standard of accommodation. The bedrooms vary considerably in style and size, but all are smart and tasteful with bold fabrics and well-equipped bathrooms. The public rooms include an elegant sitting room and cosy low-ceilinged bar. The hotel also offers very impressive cuisine.

Gravetye Manor, *East Grinstead, West Sussex, tel 01342 810567*
Described as "magical, if expensive," this creeper-clad Elizabethan manor stands in its own beautiful grounds, and boasts an oak-panelled hall and staircase, moulded plaster ceilings, and soothing bedrooms with lots of fine country house touches. Beds are decorated in traditional English style. The cooking is Michelin-starred, typical dishes being goat's cheese lasagne and hot passion fruit soufflé.

South Lodge, *Lower Beeding, Horsham, West Sussex, tel 01403 892242*
This late Victorian country house, much extended, still has huge character, with its high-beamed ceilings, oak floors and exposed stone. The bedrooms have been created with real flair, each individually styled, some with four-poster beds and all with superb bathrooms, some with jacuzzis. The Camellia Restaurant is one of a number of elegant public rooms, and the grounds are noteworthy for their fine rhododendrons and azaleas.

Newick Park, *Newick, Lewes, East Sussex, tel 01825 723633*
This delightful Grade 2 listed Georgian country house sits amid 250 acres of Sussex parkland and landscaped gardens. The spacious individually decorated bedrooms are tastefully furnished and thoughtfully equipped, with superb views. Many rooms have huge American-style kingsize beds. The comfortable public rooms include a study and elegant restaurant. The food is country-house style and there are particularly good puddings including blood orange and poppyseed cheesecake.

The Old Vicarage, *Rye, East Sussex, tel 01797 222119*
This well-established B & B is an immaculate Suffolk-pink-painted building at the top of the old town, predominantly Georgian. It boasts a cosy lounge, light wood flooring, comfortable leather sofas and a lovely window seat, and each bedroom is light, tastefully decorated and pristinely kept, with pretty colour schemes. Lavish breakfasts include home-made jams, sausages from local butchers, soda bread and warm scones.

Crossways, *Wilmington, Eastbourne, East Sussex, tel 01323 482455*
Described as a "restaurant with rooms," this blue-shuttered white-painted Georgian house is liked for its good food and excellent value. Typical dishes might include hot pigeon sausage and sesame pork schnitzel. There is no guest lounge but the rooms are equipped with fridge and TV, some of the rooms have sofas and one has a balcony. Guest comfort is described as paramount, and the AA compliment the hotel on its "excellent facilities and levels of hospitality that ensure guests return frequently."

Crossways.

TOP TEN RESTAURANTS IN SUSSEX

(Sources: AA Restaurant Guide 2005, Good Food Guide 2005)

The Gingerman, *Brighton, tel 01273 326688*

This is a cosy little restaurant in Norfolk Square, Brighton, with stripped floorboards and simple artwork. Dishes include beef meatballs with spaghetti, crispy pork belly and potato mille-feuille, red mullet with courgette linguini, hot rhubarb soufflé with custard, strawberry and white chocolate trifle, and Baileys bread and butter pudding.

One Paston Place, *Brighton, tel 01273 606933*

Set in a side street in the Kemp Town area of the city, a long light pine-floored room with many mirrors and well-spaced tables, this is described as Brighton's "star" restaurant. Dishes include crisp flaky strudel filled with truffled mushroom puree, tower of poached lobster, braised guinea fowl breast stuffed with foie gras, "melt in the mouth" roast scallops with crab tortellini and brie puree, and green apple bavarois with orange blossom ice cream.

Terre A Terre, *Brighton, tel 01273 729051*

Situated between the Pavilion and the sea, this busy and stylish eating place is described as a "peerless vegetarian restaurant;" vegetarian food is described as "taken to sublime levels on an exciting and innovative menu" with menu descriptions "like short stories." On the menu you might find roast pumpkin risotto de puy, rizola (rice patties) served with Moorish slaw, tarragon mint and flat leaf parsley, Yabba Jabba Beefy Tea (stuffed noodles), and for dessert, Cigarillo Majoolie, a fried pastry with dates, frangipane and pomegranate.

White Horse, *Chilgrove, Chichester, West Sussex, tel 01243 535219*

Although this wisteria-clad coaching inn looks very traditional from the outside, there is a contemporary look to the interior, and the menu has an excitingly modern international feel with a good range of fish specials: dishes include scallops combining with pancetta and seafood risotto, smooth, buttery, rich paprika parfait of foie de volaille coming with a cherry compote, venison steak with mandarin orange sauce and pumpkin pie, and pork loin with mushrooms and grilled shallots. The wine list, it is reported, "drips quality."

Ockendon Manor, *Cuckfield, West Sussex, tel 01444 416111*

One of the Top Ten Places To Stay in Sussex, the formal dining room of this 16th century country retreat boasts oak-panelling and stained glass windows. The cooking, it is said, "speaks with a modern French accent....timings, clear flavours and balance unite alongside an excellent interpretation of the classics." The menu might include escalope of brill with buttered Savoy cabbage, pepper-crushed beef fillet with parsnip gratin and herb butter, and classic warm apple tart Tatin with vanilla ice cream.

The White Horse at Chilgrove looks like a traditional country inn but both its interior and menu have an exciting modern feel.

Hallidays, *Funtington, Chichester, West Sussex, tel 01243 575331*
This intimate restaurant consists of three 15th century thatched and flint-walled cottages, and combines local and seasonal produce for all its dishes. The cooking style is described as uncomplicated and the food has a reputation for being honest with no pretensions. Starters might include crostini of asparagus, Parma ham and mozzarella balls, or toasted scallops with salsa rosa, main courses could include vivid saffron-sauced salmon fishcake with cucumber spaghetti, while for dessert you might be offered tonka bean and amaretto crème brulee, fine apple tart with brandied raisins, or Bavarian chocolate nut pudding.

Mirabelle at the Grand, *Eastbourne, East Sussex, tel 01323 412345*
Situated in the Grand Hotel on the seafront, the vast dining room of the Mirabelle has heavily ruched curtains, miles of flowery fabric and ornate chandeliers reminiscent of a traditional ballroom. The food is wheeled round on trolleys under silver domes, and includes piked soufflé with smoked eel sauce, cod on rosti potatoes and ratatouille, well-flavoured duck breast with sweet honeyed crust on herby potato cake, and, for dessert, Pear Tarte Tatin, a scoop of intense cinnamon ice cream on pear puree encircled by jelly cubes flavoured with pear liqueur.

***Gravetye Manor,** East Grinstead, West Sussex, tel 01342 810567*

Another of the Top Ten Places To Stay in Sussex, the restaurant with its oak panelling, candle light and log fires is a very special place. The predominantly classical ingredients, it is said, use "ambitious ingredients to bring a wow factor to many dishes." Dishes include perfectly timed scallops set on a lightly curried potato and spinach ragout and finished with parsnip froth, a succulent wild duck breast encased in feather-light pastry, and for dessert, brilliant savarin cheesecake with rhubarb.

Jeremys, Haywards Heath, West Sussex, tel 01444 441102

This restaurant is situated close to Borde Hill gardens in a converted stable block, in what is a cross between a pub and country house set within an award winning walled garden. It is described as a "model of relaxed restraint," with an elegant comfortable dining room serving stylish modern pan-European food; it is said that "strong flavours are understood and allowed full rein." The menu might include chorizo, olive and herb-stuffed squid with tomato ragout; veal kidneys in cognac; Seville orange curd mille-feuille; truffled mushroom salad with blue cheese; and a combination of pink grapefruit, orange and poached pear with sloe gin jelly.

Landgate Bistro, Rye, East Sussex, tel 01797 222829

This unpretentious restaurant, housed in two joined-together buildings just outside Rye's medieval walls, is described as "friendly, casual, honest and committed," with seasonal sourcing from a good network of good local suppliers built up over many years. Precision fish cooking is the high spot, with salmon and salt cod fishcakes that are described as "subtle" and "satisfying" while the poached fillet of turbot has been praised for its "utter simplicity." Other culinary delights include a combination of superb scallops and brill in an orange and Vermouth sauce, wild rabbit with mustard and rosemary, lemon and sherry syllabub, and Jamaican chocolate cream.

Other Books by David Bathurst

Walking the Coastline of Sussex

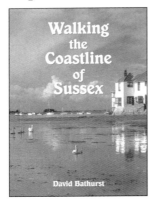

Walking Disused Railways

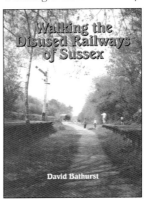

For a catalogue of other titles
please write to:
S.B. Publications
14 Bishopstone Road
Seaford
East Sussex BN25 2UB

Telephone: 01323 893498